I Know A...

When I See One

I Know a Deadbeat

Judge When I See One

Wilkenson Francois

Disclaimer

ISBN: XXXXXXXXXXXX

ISBN I3: 979-8-218-12912-5

Library of Congress Control Number: PRE000012231

Deadbeat Judge Inc: Brooklyn, NY

Dedication

For Genevieve, Who Loves Bedtime Stories,

For Esme, Who Loves to Hear Them First;

And for Non-Custodial Parents Who Miss Their

Children.

Table of Contents

Acknowledgments

This book began in my home in Brooklyn, New York, with generous input for its outline from Randall Strunk — Independent Author and Freelance Writer. I base the argument of this book on sources discovered with the help of extraordinary repositories from Hillsdale College and the dedicated people who maintain and enhance them. I especially want to thank Annie Annette, Independent Author and Freelance Writer, and Roger Carls for the helping hand with writing and supervising subsequent research and writing supported by ContentDevelopmentPro.com.

Preface

A blissful marriage quickly turns into a rocky relationship when a once loving wife makes false accusations against her husband. Karen and Ken's happy marriage falls apart when she accuses him of sexually abusing their firstborn daughter. What transpires soon afterward is draining and dramatic – a court battle involving custody of the kids, court-ordered psychosexual evaluation (PSE) against a "not arrested" entry in the system, more lies, and forging of documents by Karen's attorney. Worst of all, manipulation by a flawed court system that favors Karen, most likely because of her race.

Ken, who is of black descent, finds it hard to enjoy his rights as a father despite Child and Youth Services (CYS) finding Karen's allegations to be unfounded and unsubstantiated. It's a grueling battle as Ken deals with endless drama, thanks to Karen, who also happens to have deep-seated mental health problems.

Will he finally get to see his daughters and ever recover from the tormenting pain brought upon by this experience?

This book highlights Ken's story and exposes the corrupt judicial system that makes a particular faction of parents go through what can be termed as "modern-day slavery." Ken's story is not meant to bring you down or to gain your sympathy. Nor is it written to demonstrate how he has gone from one end of the "nice guy to an asshole" spectrum to the other and manifests male-anger against how far women have come in society.

If you give it a chance, you will see there is something in it for everyone. It creates the will to survive the most horrendous of events. It also informs affected parents about the organizations they can turn to when faced with a situation wherein the courts have the unjust power to connive against people and take away their rights.

Chapter One: The Relationship Then and Now

It was a cool evening in the bustling city of New York. Ken was particularly excited about going out because it was Friday, and he had the whole weekend off. He would spend that evening relaxing indoors and reflecting on the direction his life was taking. Later, he would go out to have a good time to ease his mind.

This 32-year-old had great dreams about the next phase of his life. He lived in his investment property in Newburgh, New York. He had just completed his Army obligations in Fort Dix, New Jersey while living with his mom in Brooklyn after moving from his own apartment in Harlem, Manhattan, New York.

After a busy week, it was time for him to unwind. That evening, Ken jubilantly marched into his best friend's apartment and threw his bag on the couch. As he settled on the sofa, Ken sighed, hoping the tiredness of a long day at work would drift away.

Jodane arrived seconds later, looking as excited as he was.

"Kenneth French!" He began. "Are you planning on staying in all night? It's Friday, remember?! You need to go out and have some fun!"

Ken sighed heavily again. "I'd really love to go, but tonight, I just want to chill out here. I've had a very exhausting day."

"That's exactly why you should party a little. You'll feel better. All drinks on me. And a cab to get us back home."

Ken stood up submissively, knowing that Jodane wouldn't take no for an answer.

"You win, bud. I'll freshen up, and then we'll be on our way out."

In an hour, they were at Row Waterfront, a plush facility in the heart of Trenton.

"We've been here so many times before," Ken said as he took a sip of his drink. "But tonight, I've noticed something different."

"Sure," Jodane agreed. "Seems like there's a party on the other side of the lounge. I must say there's a whole bevy of beautiful women. Mind if we gatecrash?"

Ken laughed. "Well, I can't resist such a display of beauty – but hold on – we don't want to leave a bad first impression!"

"I know, but we've been single for a while. Don't you think it's time we get back into the dating game?"

Jodane looked determined, but Ken was hesitant.

"Let's wait for things to work themselves out," Ken insisted. "I'm sure we'll bump into the ladies sooner or later."

"Great, I'm not in a hurry. Are you?"

"Nope."

They smiled, clinked glasses, and continued enjoying the smooth classical music. Still, Jodane couldn't help but glance toward the other side of the lounge every few minutes. Ken could tell he was very eager to catch the eye of one of the ladies. Although, Jodane wasn't that lucky because they seemed engrossed in the exclusive party.

Ken was also about to give up when his phone rang. It was his sister, and he had to get away for a moment to talk to her.

Ken hurriedly went to the back of the lounge. The phone call lasted for ten minutes. Ken's sister, Claudine, called to check in on him and seek his advice for a new business she intended to start. Ken tried convincing her that he wasn't so good at giving business advice, but she wouldn't listen. Ken wasn't even close to becoming an entrepreneur. Nevertheless, Claudine was persistent.

"You're my older brother, and you probably know more than I do."

"Ok, Claud. Let's meet tomorrow afternoon, and we'll talk about your new venture. I'm no expert, though."

Ken hung up and headed back towards the lounge. That's when he saw *her*. The most stunning woman he'd ever seen. She was gracefully walking toward him as he noticed that most of her attention was on her phone.

Ken couldn't keep himself from staring at her gorgeously petite figure, long curly hair, and flawless light skin. He gathered courage and made a decision – he would talk to her and, hopefully, get a chance to date her. Ken still had doubts in the back of his mind because of their racial differences. She was white, and he was African-American, originally from Haiti but living in America. He wondered if she would accept him the way he was without considering their racial backgrounds.

Ken ignored his unreasonable fears and waited for her to finish whatever she was doing on her phone.

Taking a step towards her, Ken smiled and stretched out his hand.

"Good evening, Miss. I'm Kenneth French. You can call me Ken."

She was somewhat taken aback, probably because of his unanticipated interest in her. Still, she smiled back at him and introduced herself.

"It's nice to meet you, Ken. I'm Karen Levy."

"You look dazzling tonight," Ken complimented her.

Her smile brightened up even more as she tried to suppress a blush.

"Thank you…um, I really have to get back to my

friend's bachelorette party."

"It's alright. I won't keep you. My friend is also waiting for me inside. But I'd love to spend some time with you before I leave tonight."

"You will," Karen assured. "We're not leaving anytime soon."

"Perfect," Ken was elated.

Karen nodded and hastily left before Ken could say anything else. He watched her fade into the lounge and made his way back in. He felt happier. Even the exhaustion that he had been feeling before was completely gone now. Seeing Karen made him feel lively and hopeful again.

Jodane was quick to point out the sudden excitement that had descended on him.

"Hey, Ken," he said. "What happened out there? Was it just Claudine's phone call, or did you meet someone?"

"I met Karen," Ken confirmed. "She's so friendly and beautiful. I'm really eager to learn more about her."

"I'm happy for you," Jodane said. "As for me, I don't seem to be so lucky tonight."

"You're up next!" Ken assured Jodane. "As soon as the formalities are over, those gorgeous ladies at the party will want to have fun, and dance, and that could be your chance. Karen also promised to see me again before we leave."

Jodane's face lit up with a smile. "That's awesome, then! I can't wait!"

They were both more excited than ever, especially Ken, as he thought about the possibility of dating Karen. After a long period of being uncertain about finding love, there he was, opening up to a new person who was so different from him and yet so friendly in a way that overshadowed their ethnic differences.

Jodane and Ken didn't have to wait for long. The bachelorette party was already nearing its end, and the ladies were now free to mingle and have fun.

As the R&B music turned up, a few ladies stepped on the dance floor.

"Come on, Jodane! This is your chance!"

"Sure! I'm certain Karen is waiting for you too!" Jodane responded.

Ken took one last sip of his drink and followed Jodane. His heart burst with excitement as he noticed Karen approaching him with a smile on her face. Ken knew she wanted to dance with him.

He took her hand. "It's amazing to see you again, Karen."

"Yes, Ken. There's something about you that I

couldn't resist. Your friendly smile, welcoming charm, and determination. Shall we dance?"

"Sure!"

They began dancing to the music. Ken looked into Karen's eyes. They were sparkling with excitement. Ken started feeling a strong affection for her. He was convinced she was falling for him too. She smiled at him. Ken smiled back. Unable to control himself, Ken leaned forward and kissed her. A wave of strong emotions ran through him. She kissed him back, and he immediately knew she had fallen for him too. Ken couldn't hide his excitement as he looked into her eyes.

"Karen, you just made me the happiest man in this lounge!"

She chuckled, amused by his apparent exaggeration, but it was true! Ken was really happy that they had found each other. "I'm happy too," she admitted. "I can't wait to see where this goes."

"Neither can I. I'm really enjoying your company. I'm glad my best friend insisted on us coming here tonight."

"We were just meant to meet tonight, that's all. I could have gone home early, but thanks to you, I'm enjoying tonight."

Karen and Ken had a lovely time at the lounge. They danced the entire night, and before parting ways, they exchanged their numbers. When Ken got home later that night, he told Jodane everything about his time with Karen. "You are one lucky guy," Jodane remarked. "To win the heart of such a beautiful girl, who happens to be white… Well, I'm not trying to be racist, but man, I admire you!"

"Don't worry, I get what you mean," Ken responded. "I know you also found someone. I saw you dancing with a pretty, curly-haired girl."

"Yes! Her name is Ella. She seemed to be a really nice and kind-hearted person. I can't wait to see her again."

Ken was happy for Jodane. Jodane had gone through a heartbreak several months ago, and to see him this cheerful and hopeful was a pleasant sight.

Thinking about his own newfound love, Ken couldn't wait for his second date with Karen. She seemed like a smart and sophisticated woman. So he wanted to get to know her closely. They promised to meet again soon to spend more time together. Ken was excited.

After staying single for a long time, the idea of being romantically involved with Karen made him so thrilled that he couldn't sleep out of excitement. He thought about all the good times they would have, the places they would visit, and what their future would be like.

Their second date was on Wednesday evening the following week. Jodane and his older brother Jean accompanied him. However, they hung out on the other side of the bar to give Karen and Ken a little room.

Karen had to commute all the way from Northeast Philadelphia to come and see Ken. The long-distance meant she was a little late for the date, so they went to a random Mexican bar that she suggested.

Ken was surprised to see that some people at the bar, specifically a waiter, a Guatemalan rock musician, and the cashier knew her. As Ken later came to learn, the musician was a friend of her Mexican ex-boyfriend, whom she hadn't mentioned before.

He felt slightly uncomfortable being in a place that may have reminded her of her past. He didn't like being in that bar, but there was nothing he could do as they were already there and had ordered drinks and food.

Was Ken being insecure? Was he worried that Karen's past may come between them? He hoped not. He silently made up his mind not to ever come to this bar again.

In the meantime, Ken tried to enjoy their date. They had limited time as Karen had a long distance to cover for home, and so Ken decided to make the most of this lucky opportunity.

Chapter Two: The Cause for Move, Settling Down, and Schooling

"I'm glad you came," Ken began with a smile. "I didn't know it was such a long drive for you."

"Distance isn't really an issue for me at the moment because you now have a special place in my heart," Karen confessed. "With time, we'll figure out what's best for us."

"I like that. I think I can confidently say that you're my girlfriend, right?"

"Right," she chuckled. "You can now tell your friends you're not single anymore."

"You too! I have really good expectations from this relationship and I can't wait to see what the future holds for us." Ken touched her hand affectionately. From the look on her face, he could tell she was happy they were together.

"How was the date?" Jean asked him as they drove back home later that night.

"Fantastic! She is so grateful that we found each other. That's what she told me. Everything is great so far!"

"I hope this goes well for you, Ken," Jodane said. "You've been single for long enough."

"Not as much as you," Ken responded with a laugh. "But I believe our time has finally come."

Karen and Ken dated for about six months before he was accepted to pursue his bachelor's degree in Information Science and Technology (IS&T) at Temple University in Philadelphia. As soon as Ken got accepted, he resigned from his job in IT, which meant that Ken had more time to spend with Karen.

Those six months were bliss for both of them. They met frequently, went to places they liked, and had fun as they established a connection with each other. Everything was going well. Even Ken's concern that Karen's past could affect their relationship was gone. He didn't notice anything strange about her.

They spent a lot of time together, and he was certain that she had forgotten about her past and was willing to make their relationship work. He decided not to think too much about who she was with before they met. They both envisioned a bright, happy future.

"I want us to have kids one day," Ken told Karen as they enjoyed the cool evening breeze in a New York park. "A happy family is what I've always dreamt of."

"It has been my dream too since I was a little girl," Karen assured him. "And because I love you, I'd be so happy if we had kids of our own."

"We will," Ken assured her as he gave her an affectionate embrace. They both had similar hopes for the future, which was a good thing.

Karen was as ambitious as him, hoping to climb the ladder of success in her medical career as a Spanish Interpreter. She had graduated from Temple University with a Spanish and Portuguese degree in Latin American Studies.

A little while after Ken started his bachelor's degree at Temple University, he moved into Karen's apartment in the Fox Chase neighborhood of Northeast Philadelphia. It was great to stay with someone he knew and loved. The chemistry between them strengthened as they established a deeper bond. They even talked about marriage in the near future.

For the first time since Ken started dating, this was the only relationship that was going really great so far. His relationship with Karen helped him forget his disappointing past. He could now properly focus on his relationship, his studies, and their future together.

They both lived comfortably because Ken's post-9/11 VA benefits covered both the tuition fees and the cost of living. He provided everything they needed so Karen could pursue her own goals without any financial pressure. Ken always tried to take time out to go out with her. He didn't want to let anything come between them. He had found the love of his life, and he would do anything possible to help their romance thrive.

"I'd like you to meet my mom one day," Ken told Karen a couple of months later. "I've told her a lot about you, and she's so eager to see you."

"Sure, we can plan that. That's fine by me," Karen agreed, although she appeared surprised. It was as if she did not want to meet his mother just yet. Ken thought Karen was just nervous, especially since she wasn't sure how his mother would react when she learns they are from different races.

Ken hadn't told his mom about their racial differences. He couldn't care less about it because he knew his mom didn't care about racial or cultural differences either. As long as Karen and Ken were getting along well together, that's what really mattered.

The same week, Ken told his mother that he and Karen would be visiting her over the weekend. She was glad to finally meet the woman he loved.

"Mom is friendly and easygoing," Ken reminded Karen as they left the apartment. "Don't feel nervous or out of place. My brother and sister already know about you, and they like you."

"I hope so… I hope that you're not just saying this to make me feel better." Karen said. By the time they arrived at his mother's house, all her nervousness was gone, and she comfortably interacted with his mother, his sister, Claudine, and his brother, Jean.

"I'm happy for you," Claudine said to Karen. "My brother is really honest and caring. It's not easy to find such good men nowadays."

"True," Karen agreed. "I consider myself very lucky to have found him."

"And we are glad he met a gorgeous and humble girl like you," Jean added. "You two are the perfect match."

Karen blushed. "Thank you for saying such nice words about us."

"You're the right woman for my son, Karen," his mother said. "I've not seen him so happy in a long time."

Karen seemed to be flattered by his mother's words. She was very grateful for all the nice things that his family had to say about her. They had dinner, and soon after, it was time for them to go back.

"I'd also love to meet your family," Ken said a few days later, noticing that she wasn't so keen on him getting to know her family. Perhaps she wasn't ready. Or maybe she felt like everything was happening too fast. For Ken, it really wasn't so. It had been almost a year since they had met, and were now living together. Two weeks later, she finally agreed to take him to her mother's place.

The reception was good, and Ken was really happy when he saw that her mother, Misha, was very welcoming from the moment she laid eyes on him. Although Karen wasn't as happy as he was, she still managed to smile and act as if everything was okay.

Ken met Karen's younger brother Noah too. He was especially talkative and made him feel comfortable throughout the evening.

Ken later came to learn that Noah was a sous-chef at a few restaurants. He frequented New York and happened to be around for the weekend when Ken and Karen were visiting. Noah was very nice and friendly. He even let them stay in his studio for one of the many weekends when they visited.

As Ken got to know more about Karen's background, he discovered that she hated her mom. This was evident throughout their relationship and was apparently because she blamed her mother for her parents' bloody divorce, which led to her father getting diagnosed with diabetes. He got very sick from drinking all the time, which eventually led to his death.

Karen always left her father's wedding ring hanging on the door hinge at their apartment, even when her mother visited. She actually wanted to continue her father's legacy since he used to do the same after he divorced Karen's mother. Ken somehow managed to convince her to take the ring down as her mother had expressed discontentment for doing so.

It wasn't easy for Karen to let go of the resentment against her mother. She would sometimes give her the cold shoulder when she visited. However, Ken pitied her mom because she seemed to be a kindhearted woman. He knew he couldn't force Karen to love her mom. So he decided to give her some time.

The most important thing was that they truly loved one another and had big plans for the future.

Chapter Three: Army Reserves — Outgoing/Incoming Unit Transfer

Shortly after Ken moved into Karen's apartment in Philadelphia, they went to an army function called Army Strong Bonds. The objective of the event was to build strong relationships between couples. This was just after he was transferred to a new Army Unit from New York.

The function turned out to be really good for them as they bonded together and enjoyed the different fun activities there. Ken particularly enjoyed the field excursion that all participants had to take part in to win. They both didn't care much about winning, except for being taken away by all the beautiful things Virginia had to offer in the vicinity of nice beaches, restaurants, parks, and hotels.

This was one of the best experiences they had ever had. They were in love and were having the best time together. Except for a few challenges every couple goes through, Ken could confidently say they were doing well. He was certain they would grow together and spend the rest of their lives as a perfect couple.

After a year of being together, Ken took a big step forward. He took Karen to one of their favorite beaches, and they spent most of their afternoon there. They enjoyed exotic seafood at a nearby restaurant and then went home to spend the rest of the evening together. They watched the sunset as they stood on the balcony.

As the cool evening breeze blew, Karen's hair swayed in response. She looked at Ken with a smile on her face as he thought to himself that she was more beautiful than ever. "I've never had such a good time with anyone," she revealed. "Now I know I made the right choice to be with you."

"I feel the same way," Ken replied. "We've had our ups and downs, but in the end, love wins. Your presence makes me feel complete. It's like I've found a part of me I never knew I needed. You always bring a smile on my face, Karen, and that's why…."

Ken got down on one knee and took a ring out of his pocket. "I want to spend the rest of my life with you. Will you marry me, Karen?"

The proposal was a huge surprise for her. Her face lit up with excitement as she had a big grin from ear to ear on her face. She responded excitedly, "Yes, I will!"

With happiness overflowing through Ken, he put the ring on her finger, got up on his feet, embraced her tightly, and kissed her. "This is the happiest day of my life"! My love for you will never end."

"Mine too," she said excitedly as tears of happiness ran down her cheeks. "I'm now sure that you're committed to making everything we dreamed of a reality."

"I am, Karen. From the first day I met you, I

realized that you're different and one of a kind. That day I decided to never let you go, and tonight, I've made sure of it."

"All my uncertainties about the future are gone," Karen said. "There was a time I thought you were just like other guys that I used to know, but now I know that you're all in. That makes me love you even more." Another kiss from her assured Ken that her love for him was true.

Ken had gone to a ring store not too far from Philadelphia, where they once lived, just so he could get the ring that Karen once mentioned that she liked very much.

During this time, Ken later discovered that Karen was trying to find out what he was doing. She checked their joint checking account and knew that he had bought the ring.

They decided that their wedding would be within two weeks. However, they ended up getting married within a week. They both agreed there was no need to spend a fortune on the wedding. They realized that many people who get married lavishly end up in debt after all the glamor.

Their wedding only cost them $3,000. They believed that the love they had for each other was what truly mattered. They could never put a price on it. So they opted to keep it simple.

Karen's aunt, Nahe Flicke, was an Ordained Minister, and she was happy to endorse the marriage certificate after they went to the City Hall. They changed their plan of inviting 20 people from each side of the family to just 10. The wedding ceremony was really small and held in her mother's backyard. Afterward, they celebrated with everyone at the Yardley Inn.

They had reached another level in their relationship. Ken was happier than he'd ever been since he met her. He was really proud of himself for taking this bold step. His time to be deployed in a new Army Unit in Afghanistan was nearing. So he had felt it necessary to marry Karen. He didn't want her to think that he didn't love her or didn't take their relationship seriously enough.

While he was in Afghanistan, Karen would frequently call and text. She would often complain about missing him too much. Ken also missed her a lot. She was the love of his life, but there was nothing he could do about it. All they could do was stay in touch through their phones and wait until his deployment was over. Only then could they see each other again.

Upon his return to the States the following year, Ken couldn't help but hold grudges against Karen because of her constant whining. He felt as if she was putting a lot of pressure on him.

After settling down for a few months, Ken learned to outgrow his grudges and rekindle his love for

Karen. He made an effort to do all the things they used to do before his deployment. Ken knew that harboring these grudges would eventually cause bitterness in his heart and ultimately have a negative effect on their relationship, which was the last thing that he wanted. So he let those grudges remain in the past and dedicated his time to making~~make~~ their love work.

Chapter Four: Post-Deployment Reintegration Challenges & Family Planning

Although Ken was committed to making their relationship work, it wasn't easy to get rid of the resentment that had built up while he was away in Afghanistan. He had always felt like Karen was unreasonable, and that she didn't want to understand their situation at that time.

Sometimes, Ken wondered if she was just being selfish. Maybe all she cared about was him being there for her. She didn't understand that Ken was working and he had no control over where he would be deployed. As Ken thought about all this, he fought hard to let go of the resentment. Fortunately, it all faded away with time as they went out for dinner dates and did what they loved together.

Ken was even happier when his family organized a welcome home party for him. They had a great time reuniting after so many days away. Families from both sides got to interact with each other.

Ken and Karen's mothers got along really well. This was evident from the day they first got to know each other. Ken noticed that on that particular day, Karen's attitude towards her mother was better. Despite Karen's indifference, Ken hoped the hatred she had harbored for so long would soon be drowned by all the love and concern her mother showed.

Ken had also invited a few friends to the party, including Jodane and Pierre. They were excited to see him for the first time in several months.

"Weekends were not the same without you, Ken," Pierre told him over a drink. "We did have fun, but it could have been better if you were around."

"I appreciate that, bud. Nights out are always a blast with you guys, but I had to work, you know."

"We understand that," Jodane said. "The good thing is that you're back now. Let's look forward to greater times ahead."

"Sure, guys," Ken said, raising his glass. "Let's toast to that!"

After the party and a long, much-needed rest that night, Ken focused on adjusting to life back home. He returned to work after a few days. His expectations for the future were big. They were well-settled, and he figured that this was the right time for them to start a family.

Ken talked to Karen about it one evening after returning home from work. He could see the hesitant look on her face as she tried to give him an explanation.

"You know I've been using birth control pills," she began. "I've also been suffering from endometriosis, and I've had to go through years of treatment. I'm not sure if this is the right time for us to have kids."

"You're fine, my love," Ken told her. "I haven't seen you complaining of pain like you used to. But let's take it easy. I don't want to feel like I'm pressuring you."

Karen smiled, relieved. "Thanks, honey. Like I told you once, I really want us to have kids someday. I haven't changed my mind about that, don't worry."

Ken stayed patient with Karen. For some time, the thought of having kids was not so heavy on his mind. They went on with their routine lives and showed love for one another in the best ways they knew. Every time they made love, he reminded Karen how much he cared for her. She assured him the same and it allowed them to navigate through the ups and downs of marriage.

One day, when Ken was sitting on the couch, Karen was anxiously walking around in the apartment. He didn't realize that this day would be the beginning of the most overwhelming difficulties he would have to deal with during the course of his relationship with Karen.

"Ken, I think you should go and stay with your

friend Pierre," Karen said.

"Why do you say that?" Ken asked, puzzled. At first, he thought she was kidding. But her answer shocked him and got him really angry.

"I'm not a good woman for you!"

Ken noticed the seriousness on her face, and at once, he knew she wasn't kidding. Her words made him so upset that he slammed the door on her face and left. Ken drove off to town to meet Pierre at Parx Casino. He ratted everything out to Pierre. He was astonished to hear all of this. He didn't know what the right thing would be to say but he told Ken that he would keep him company for as long as he needed. Ken admitted that he didn't feel comfortable going back home. That meant they would spend most of the night at the casino.

Until the next morning, Ken was either winning or losing his money without a care in the world. He had his phone off the whole time he was at the casino and didn't turn it back on until the next morning.

As soon as he turned his phone on, he got so many voicemails from Karen. She said she was sorry and that she had called the cops regarding his whereabouts since he was nowhere to be found.

"I miss you. You should come home!" Ken couldn't tell if she was sincere or just desperate for him to return home.

Eventually, Ken returned home. However, the air was filled with tension. No matter how many times Karen apologized for what she had said, he still had doubts about what she truly felt about him.

After all the blissful times they had spent together, Ken never thought, even for a second, that she would utter the words that forced him to spend the night away from home and the woman he loved.

He started to think that perhaps there was a bigger problem that had led her to blurt such things out. Ken called her mother, Misha, and her husband, Sam, to discuss Karen's unusual behavior.

He told them that he'd like to have a family intervention so Karen would get help with whatever she was going through. However, her mom reminded Ken that she had a bad relationship with Karen throughout her life, ever since her ugly divorce from her dad. Misha didn't want to jeopardize the somewhat good mother and daughter relationship they had now. Ken understood her situation and agreed not to go ahead with the intervention.

A few weeks later, Ken found out that Karen was pregnant with their firstborn. They both cried. It's the most overwhelming feeling for a man to get the news of becoming a father. One of his biggest dreams ever since they met was coming true.

Ken was hopeful that Karen would be more cautious with this new responsibility. He also had a huge responsibility ahead of him to support and encourage her. He also hoped she would seek help to overcome whatever mental issues she had been dealing with. Even if she found it difficult to fully open up to Ken, it was best to get help for the sake of their baby.

Chapter Five: Married with Children, Home Ownership, and College Graduation

It had been over a decade since Ken and Karen's firstborn daughter was conceived. It was around that time when the Senate passed the military medical malpractice law. While on active duty in the U.S. army between 2007 and 2009, Ken almost didn't have his two girls because of an outside clinic's attempt to perform a vasectomy against his medical consult for circumcision. He had the option to use Army funds for a medical operation relay added to circumcision.

However, the medical staff would have gotten themselves into medical malpractice had he not read the medical consult carefully. They actually had him down for a vasectomy. He was relieved from the trauma of infertility forever. Imagine how crushed he would have been if the medical staff had actually gone through with the vasectomy and the lengths that he would go to in order to get compensated by the clinic.

Needless to say, Ken focused on the present. Karen was expecting, and she needed all the support Ken could give. At first, he didn't pressure her into seeking a psychological evaluation. He believed she was mature and wise enough to realize that if she really needed help, it was necessary to consult a professional.

As Ken went through the joy of being a father, he couldn't help but notice that Karen started getting quite anxious. This didn't appear like the general anxiety that soon-to-be parents usually experience. It was as if Karen was worried about something.

"Are you okay?" Ken asked her one morning after breakfast.

"Yes, I'm fine. Do I look like I'm not fine?"

Her response sounded a bit irrational, but Ken brushed that aside. "You look anxious and I'm concerned."

"It's the usual anxiety that any new mother has." Karen avoided his gaze as she spoke.

"I don't think so, honey," Ken said firmly. "I think you need to see a psychologist."

"What?! Are you implying that I'm crazy?"

"No. You're mistaken, honey. Anyone can have a mental health problem. It doesn't mean they are crazy. It means they are human, and they need help."

Karen wouldn't see any sense in what Ken was saying. She stormed out of the room and locked herself in the bedroom, crying. Ken felt bad because he felt he had made her mood worse, which wasn't his intention. He only wanted her to get evaluated and get treatment or therapy so she could be okay.

Now here he was, sighing and wondering what approach he should have used to make sure she didn't overreact. Ken tried opening the bedroom door, but it didn't budge.

"Karen, please open up! I didn't mean to make you feel bad about yourself. We can talk about this without getting mad at each other."

After much persuasion, Karen finally opened the door and agreed to talk. "I went for a check-up yesterday and everything was okay, except…." She paused, and this made Ken anxious.

"Except what, Karen? Whatever it is, I'll be by your side to take care of you."

Ken's words encouraged her to open up, although the information she gave him was not so good. She handed Ken the medical report as she spoke.

"I just discovered that I'm a carrier of both Gaucher and Tay Sachs diseases, as a result of stemming from the Eastern European Jew lineage. I'm scared of what this could mean for our unborn baby. Slowed development, allergies, and who knows what else. I also want you to go through some DNA tests, considering you're a Haitian of French descent. You may have Eastern European Jew ancestors too. Our kids could inherit such diseases if we are both 50% positive each."

This report broke Ken. But he knew he had to be strong for his firstborn. She was innocent and loved. The best thing they could do as her parents would be to ensure she was well taken care of, even before she came into this world.

"Alright, I'll take a DNA test," Ken said. "Don't let this worry you. I don't think I'm a carrier of these diseases. I believe our baby will be fine."

Karen cheered up a little. She was able to get on with her daily routine, and Ken went to work an hour late.

Later that afternoon, he found time to figure out how to take the test. Ken tried to have his insurance company cover the medical costs, but it turned out that unless the applicant was a pregnant woman, they were out of luck. He informed Karen about the situation, and she was devastated.

She was so focused on making him take the test that she couldn't concentrate on anything else. She even started suspecting that Ken was a carrier, even though he had assured her he wasn't. He started feeling uneasy, knowing that without insurance, he was not in a position to pay for the test. Then, he thought of something.

The only way to grant Karen's wish was to ask the Veterans Affairs (VA) Medical Center to cover the medical bills. After his persistence, Ken's attempts were successful, and he was able to get the test done.

He anxiously waited for the results, hoping that he would prove Karen's suspicions false. The results came back negative. Ken was not a carrier. He was extremely relieved and happy. When he told Karen the good news, her anxiety levels went down. She even apologized for suspecting him.

"I'm sorry that I had such solid suspicions. I was just worried about our baby." She apologized.

"I'm not mad at you, dear. I totally understand."

Ken expected Karen to be calmer now that they had sorted out the DNA issue. However, that wasn't the case. It turned out that she had deep-seated mental issues that would cause undesirable tension in their marriage.

One evening Ken witnessed Karen grinding her teeth and banging her head against the kitchen wall while holding a knife. Ken was expecting her to be preparing dinner at that time. When he went to check on her and found her in this alarming state, his suspicions about her mental health were confirmed.

"Sweetheart, what's going on?" Ken inquired,

not sure whether to take the knife away from her or to let her get back to her senses first. She was shocked to see Ken standing there. It was as if she hadn't expected him to show up and catch her in that state.

She began trembling as she clenched the knife more tightly. And Ken knew better than to try and take it from her.

"Please try to calm down, honey," he continued. "You're going to be okay. I understand what you're going through is not easy."

"How can you possibly understand what I'm going through?" Karen cried bitterly. "Do you know what it feels like to be the reason your child could have life-long health problems?"

"I may not exactly know how it feels, but I can assure you that our baby will do great. It's not your fault that you're a carrier. We'll give our baby the best care and she'll grow up to be a healthy and happy girl."

Ken was relieved when Karen calmed down. She stopped trembling, although she was still holding the knife.

"Please put the knife down," Ken told her. "I don't want you to hurt yourself."

It took a while for Karen to get back to her

senses. After their meal, Ken couldn't keep himself from telling her the truth, no matter how ugly it sounded.

"I think you have a problem, dear, and you need to see a professional."

"It's not that serious, darling," Karen tried to brush it off again. "It was just an episode of anxiety. I've been handling such episodes for some time now. I've always been able to control them."

"What about the knife?" Ken reminded her. "Don't you think you could have done something dangerous if I hadn't come in time?"

"No, I don't think so. You very well know I was whipping up a meal for us. So it's understandable that I was holding the knife."

"I see. But please consider talking to a therapist. Even mild anxiety can develop into something serious."

"I will. I'm just not ready to open up to a stranger."

Ken could see that this conversation would eventually turn into an argument, so he didn't comment further on the issue. The rest of Karen's pregnancy had no major issues, except for the normal symptoms that most pregnant women experience. Ken accompanied her to the doctor's appointments as much as he could. And when it was time for Baby GO to be born, he was present at the hospital.

Ken was overwhelmed with joy when he held his lovely daughter for the first time. She was beautiful and healthy, and the parents were thankful for her safe delivery.

Everything was good for the first few days but after some time, Karen's sporadic behavior recurred. She would have frequent mood swings and behave irrationally. Ken insisted that therapy was necessary, but she continued brushing off his advice until Baby GO was four months old.

Afterward, she revealed to Ken what was keeping her from seeking a psychological evaluation.

"I'm afraid that if the psychologist finds out something is wrong with me, they may take away our baby. To make it worse, my mind is always thinking that one day, the building will burn down to the ground. I can't imagine losing our baby. Not now. Not ever."

Ken couldn't stand the thought that Karen had a problem, and she wasn't on board with the idea of getting it checked. He knew that ignoring her condition could possibly put all of their lives in danger. It was really hard to get the sight of her holding a knife and trembling uncontrollably out of his mind.

Finally, her constant whining put Ken over the edge, and he had no choice but to force her to go for an evaluation. She realized Ken was very serious this time and eventually decided to consult with a "Talk Therapist" on their insurance plan.

After her first appointment, Karen showed a "good wife" attitude around the house. Even Ken became less stressed as he was too busy working and putting food on the table. Her improved behavior and attitude werewas a huge relief as he had been so worried about their overall well-being as a young family.

Ken was happy to see Karen offer support and strength to him for the emotional endurance that he had to bear because of immense emotional and psychological pain. However, everything did not turn out perfectly.

As Baby GO hit growth milestones and the months progressed, their doctor informed them that she had Food Protein Induced Enterocolitis Syndrome (FPIES), a form of food allergy their second-born daughter, Essie, would also have when she became a toddler.

Although Karen's attitude had improved, she still wasn't as stable as Ken needed her to be. She was seeking help like he had told her to, but she would switch from one behavioral health psychologist to another, citing lack of direction as the reason.

This made Ken wonder whether she wasn't getting the help she needed, or she hadn't found a professional who understood her. He also knew that jumping from one psychologist to another wasn't healthy. So he told her to decide what she felt was best for her and stick to one professional.

"I will be okay," Karen kept assuring Ken, seeing how concerned he was for her mental health.

"Our kids and I need you to be okay," Ken said. "I genuinely care about you. That's why I can't stand watching you go through this alone."

"I don't feel alone, honey," Karen insisted. "I have you, and even though you're mostly busy at work, you always make an effort to support me."

While Karen appeared to be doing better than in the previous months, Ken wanted her to be able to overcome all her problems. Whether he was around or not, his family's safety was very important to him.

She later proved that she had finally found a psychologist who understood her. She showed him some paperwork that mentioned the kind of therapy she was getting and her scheduled appointments. So he finally stopped worrying and got to focus on work fully without the fear of something going wrong when he was not around.

They had goals to achieve as a couple, and at the top of their list was buying a family home. It didn't turn out to be as easy as they expected. When they went to buy their first home together in Willow Grove, Pennsylvania, they ran into many problems with the first and well-known banks within the military rank structure. They were not qualified enough for USAA's VA Loan due to a K-1 Form associated with Karen's late dad's trucking business that her mom inherited in alimony.

The bank refused to approve the loan because the business-generated K-1 form was under a certain tax structure. This was a huge challenge for them, but fortunately, they managed to secure a family home.

They settled down and hired a babysitter straight out of high school. She watched their kids when they were at work. They trusted her completely and didn't have anything to worry about, as she did a good job from the beginning.

Then one day, the unexpected happened. She was watching Baby GO in the living room while Essie was sleeping in the master bedroom. Apparently, Essie being one and a half years old had woken up from sleep and tried to climb down the bed. This happened when the babysitter was busy watching TV with Baby GO and didn't hear Essie calling for help. She tried to climb down the bed and ended up falling on her head.

Exhausted from work, Ken had just walked into the house. He was supposed to nap for a few hours and head right back to work that day. He was panicking badly, worrying that Essie could have been badly hurt. So he checked on her to examine her contusion and determine whether the injury was serious.

He figured that Essie was fine, although she continued to appear hurt whenever he looked at her.

"You're going to be fine, sweetheart," Ken told her. He embraced her, which apparently made her feel better. To Ken, it was just an accident, and he didn't want to be too quick to blame the babysitter much.

However, Karen was furious with her. A few days later, he learned that the sitter was gone within 60 seconds. Regardless of Ken's initial assessment, Karen had taken Essie to the hospital when she came home while he was asleep. The doctor told them that the baby was fine when Ken woke up and went to the clinic after just getting 2 hours of sleep.

He believed that this was a waste of insurance funds for the hospital. But they were better off that way rather than being sorry for their sweet little Essie if something were to go wrong.

That same gone-in-60-seconds scenario goes

way back to the firing of a Grub Burger Bar waitress after Karen had reported an incident to the manager. Karen did share with Ken that she complained to the Grub manager about the waitress' poor choice of words and that she "probably would not fit at this table" for obvious reasons that she was pregnant with Essie at the time. Ken could not have done anything to stop the waitress from getting terminated, especially when the manager had given the family a coupon to eat for FREE on the next visit.

Ken soon graduated with a B.S. Degree from Temple University. This was a major achievement for him, and he anticipated a better future with a more stable income. Little did he know that what lay ahead was nothing that he expected.

Chapter Six: Maintaining a Balance with Army Reserves, Career, and Family

Like Ken anticipated, there was a new career opportunity for him right after graduating. While maintaining a balance between the Army Reserves, his career, and his family, he often deprived himself of sleep as he had late work schedules.

However, he considered this a better opportunity for career progression and family balance. Despite his busy schedule, he learned to establish a work-life balance and spent enough time with his wife and daughters.

Ken had no idea that Karen's mental health was declining again until some really dramatic events began to take place. These events would later ruin their marriage. He had lost his trust in Karen, especially because Karen gossiped with friends and family. He was angry that the marriage he had hoped would last forever was slowly turning out to be really turbulent.

At first, Karen suspected Ken was having an affair with her childhood friend, Lizzie's younger sister, Drew, who she thought looked like a model. She had been quite jealous of her looks, and it showed as Ken had a long conversation with Drew.

They had been talking at the bar where everyone was celebrating Lizzie's bachelorette party. A few days later, while Karen sat in the driver's seat to take the kids to a playground, she went on an emotional rollercoaster, which caught Ken off-guard.

"There is something I need to know, Ken. Are you having an affair with Drew? I saw the way you were talking to her and I got suspicious."

The question completely caught him off guard. He was baffled. For a minute, Ken said nothing. After a long silence, he finally answered.

"No, Karen. You got it wrong. I don't play where I eat. I especially don't have anything to do with your friends."

These suspicions were completely baseless because Ken wasn't the type of person who would let anything ruin their relationship. When sexual intercourse was painful for Karen due to the hormonal changes happening inside her throughout her second pregnancy, Ken even considered using lotion bottles instead of cheating on her.

Would you consider this approach a way to resurrect your marriage from the kiss of death? Even if they had their difficult moments, they always worked it out.

However, at this point, it seemed the difficult times outnumbered the good ones. Ken was so furious that Karen would even accuse him of such a thing.

During this time, he found it hard to love her the way he used to. The air between them became cold, and they were no longer happy like they used to be.

Karen went as far as to take advice from friends on how to get Ken to make love to her. He later found out that this was due to the lack of sexual intimacy in their marriage.

Karen always used to talk about it to random strangers. She would ask for their opinion on her concerns and tried to get their validation. It was a little too much to share with outsiders. And the worst part was that she didn't have any problem with doing so. She wouldn't even stop when Ken told her to.

She didn't even respect the boundaries of their private marriage life. Once Karen forgot to log out from their elder daughter's phone and Ken caught her sharing their personal affairs with her friends.

Another time, on their way back from a family getaway in Cape May, New Jersey, she told Ken that she'd asked her male friend, James, about how and when she should have sex with Ken. She explained it by saying that they hadn't had sexual intercourse for a while now. However, they had already agreed upon this since they couldn't find enough time to be together because of work and kids. They had agreed to do it once on the first of every month.

Ken was enraged by Karen's confession, and he eventually grew tired of her sharing their personal marital affairs with her friends and family.

She continued to complain even when he kept his word to make the necessary amends. Ken strongly believed that the issues concerning their marriage were private. And if they both couldn't come to an agreement, it would be better to go for counseling.

Ken started feeling numb in his hopelessly broken marriage as he had to put up with Karen's behavior. He felt like Karen was a completely different person now. She was slowly turning into a stranger and it was heartbreaking.

He knew their marriage was nearly broken as Karen's behavior had changed around the house. She had lost Ken's trust because he felt he could no longer share his secrets with her. He kept all of them to himself, afraid that things may go south if he opened up to her.

She always gossiped with her friends and acted on whatever they told her to do. She attempted to make a scene on the street once and yelled at Ken for the things she needed help with around the house. However, all this drama could've been avoided if she had had a mature conversation with him. Ken was really embarrassed and warned her not to repeat this act ever again. The last thing he wanted was their personal matters being paraded in public.

It just wasn't healthy for their relationship as it had filled her heart with hateful feelings. All the gossiping made it feel like she had married her friends. Over the years, Karen had become a hateful wife overlooking the 'dos and don'ts of marriage'. And worst of all, she had become painfully numb. She didn't realize that her actions were slowly crushing their marriage and ending the true love they used to have for each other. Their marital life was no longer joyful like it used to be.

With other people's encouragement, Karen developed strong feelings of pseudo-feminism and felt pressured to go against Ken.

Once, she revealed that her friend, Alyssa, told her that Bob was more of a feminist than Ken. Karen would say such things in hopes that Ken would react to her rhetoric. However, Ken saw her manipulation tactics from a mile away. Karen had started watching shows like The Handmaid's Tale, which furthered her feelings of pseudo-feminism.

She was always meeting Lilly Howard next door, whose husband was Ken's acquaintance. Ken later learned they would watch shows about married women going to jail for doing bad things to their husbands. Anyhow, Karen had been making snarky comments about the opposite sex. She conflated other people's perceived alliance with the feminist movement with his perceived lack thereof, especially when she shared Alyssa's thoughts with Ken at the dinner table.

She went on and on and asked Ken, "Is that what my life is going to be like? This woman at Bob's birthday party told me that all that she'd been doing since her divorce was sleeping with younger men behind dumpsters?!"

Ken was shocked to find out how self-sabotaging her thoughts were. What discouraged him, even more, even more was the fact that she didn't make any efforts to make their marriage work. She continued making things worse as the days passed.

Several times during their encounters at home, Karen would say dumb things to win an argument. Once when talking about their own safety to avoid any break-ins, Karen argued, "Why would you want to have a gun in the house knowing how my mental health is?" Ken thought her remarks were irrational because he had always insisted on getting professional help. He was always ready to support her in her journey toward recovery.

While he was thinking of ways to protect his home and family, she imagined the worst that could happen with a gun in the house. Ken knew that a gun was not the only thing in their house that could cause any harm. There were all sorts of things like knives and lighters that could harm the house. He thought of the knife incident in the kitchen, it dawned on him how weak Karen's mental state was. She was unreasonable and irrational. This made him lose all his hopes for a happy marriage.

When discussing how Ken's work had become too overwhelming for her, Karen would say, "All you do at work is drink coffee!"

In another instance, fueled by her pseudo-feminist thoughts, she told Ken, "You should watch The Handmaid's Tale."

She was always bitching about all the house chores she had to do with her friends. "Is this only my kitchen, and am I supposed to do all the cooking? Why doesn't he cook?!"

Once, Karen revealed to Ken that she had told

her shrink how he tried sticking a finger up her butt during sex, despite her saying no multiple times. Ken was utterly shocked as this was far from the truth. She would always distort the truth.

Karen never had his best interests in mind the way he did. At one point, she made fun of Ken taking his multivitamins and acted as if she cared about what goes into her body, while in reality, her contradictory actions showed otherwise. She had her exes lined up at the GNC store for "*vitamins.*"

This made it clear to him that Karen's mental health needed serious attention, and if he weren't strong enough, she would make him lose control of his own feelings. His patience was on edge. His emotions were hurt. He tried to take it one day at a time, hoping that maybe one day she would care about saving their marriage and act differently. Sadly, she didn't.

He could see that Karen was immensely frustrated and couldn't let it out the way he could as a man. It was unsurprising to Ken that she thought that monogamy was a double-standard idea while dating, as women were attracted to a man who had many women interested in him. Karen immediately reacted to that frustrated energy and sexual excitement from his rhetoric, saying once over a family dinner that they ought to spice things up with swinging in their marriage.

She then got Ken to dance to a song, thereby suspecting he was a one-woman man. A few days later, Ken looked up the nearby clubs and pinned Karen in one of them, but she showed grace by sharing photos of their two daughters. Karen was no less than a test in his life. And as the legendary comedian Dave Chapelle would say, "Gotcha bitch!"

Chapter Seven: Children and Youth Services (CYS) Labeled the Allegations of Child Abuse Unfounded and Unsubstantiated

What followed next were false allegations of child abuse. After everything they had been through as a couple, Karen pinned these allegations on Ken while he was away for the weekend for an Army Battle Assembly. This came as a devastating shock to him.

How could he abuse his own daughters, who he dearly loved? Ken had always feared that her mental issues could lead to something incredibly horrible. But this was just too much. He wished that it was a nightmare. But sadly, it wasn't. It was a reality that he had to face and deal with.

To him, these allegations marked the end of their marriage. Ken couldn't take the distress he was going through any longer. He had been patient and supportive for long enough, but the situation continued to get worse. There had been too many red flags he chose to ignore and remain optimistic about their future.

He had put up with her random outbursts, gossip, and all the disagreements she had with him. These were all the signs that any man would consider a tipping point, but love is truly blind, and he held onto it until their continuing years into the marriage. It was now evident that Karen wanted to be all alone and didn't want to make any efforts to save their marriage. Ken was convinced that she was determined to end it. The imminent end was certainly bound to be ugly because there was no way he could remain silent over the accusations or even accept false claims against himself.

On Saturday, March 10th, 2018, Karen called Ken to inform him that she had called Child Protective Services (CPS) to tell them that he had sexually abused their three-year-old daughter, Baby GO. He got very furious at this insane accusation.

"What did you do, Karen? Have you lost your mind? You're on your own now!"

Later, he learned from the Abington Police detective that he was in their home with Karen's friend, Lizzie, and her husband, Darrell, and that's when his attorney showed up for an affidavit. With Karen's irrational behavior in and out of their home and her baseless report to the CPS, Abington Police, and District Attorney, divorce was imminent and would mark an end to their marriage.

They got married on June 24th, 2012. Their two lovely daughters, Baby GO and Essie, meant the world to him. When the marriage was intact, they lived in their sweet home in Willow Grove, Pennsylvania.

Six years later, on March 12th, 2018, Ken filed for Support and Custody of their daughters upon Karen's false allegations made on March 10th, 2018, to tarnish his reputation and relationships. Upon being contacted on March 12th, CYS advised Ken to temporarily move out of the home for their own investigation.

On April 2, 2018, after he temporarily stayed with a friend in Philadelphia, he agreed to pay for childcare, support, mortgage, dental and health insurance, and auto insurance for the vehicles that both Karen and he used (the Honda and Toyota, respectively). He agreed to pay for all of this until the divorce was final, as Karen's insufficient earnings and her history of mental health would make it hard for her to take care of the girls.

Following a petition for modification during the Support Hearing on October 18th, 2018, which was declared "Complex" by Judge Coacher, Ken filed an exception on February 11th, 2019, to Hon. Judge Patricia Coacher's Finding of Facts of the February 08th, 2019 Order. That's because the Master erred in determining his income by failing to hold him to his prior income when he didn't get his Army Reserves to pay on October 25, 2018. This was due to the honorable discharge and exhaustion of his unemployment benefits.

Hon. Sr. Judge Emanuel Bertin showed total disregard for the sufficient evidence already provided by Ken preceding all the conference proceedings and hearings on May 3rd, 2019. But later, he vacated Judge Coacher's order to replace the April 2nd, 2018 Order, which showed an appearance of partiality.

In early April of 2018, thorough vetting by criminal law enforcement and various government agencies, they failed to confirm Karen's allegations. Ken stood firm in his truth because he only wanted the best for his daughters. He didn't care how many times he was interrogated. What mattered the most was the truth. He freely presented himself for every vetting procedure and stood his ground.

Moreover, the same kind of interrogations by the Domestic Relations Office ensued during a scheduled Contempt Compliance Conference on March 7th, 2019, and revealed that the Enforcement Officer had no reasonable basis to find probable cause. However, they would continue harassing Ken upon Hon. Judge Carolyn T. Carluccio's request, asking if there was any down payment on the purchase of his new 2019 Jeep Cherokee. He had every reason to believe there was a silver lining behind the onslaught of discrimination in C.P. Montgomery County Court, especially when all those involved in both the matters of Custody and Support appeared to risk creating perceptions of partiality.

HEARING OFFICER: "Look, I'm—I'm—I'm not getting into that. I'm not involved in the custody. I'm a numbers cruncher, that's all I am and if that is the basis of your objection, okay, to—to the initial."

This further shows that this was just an industry of pretentious judges gaslighting the accused and making parents hire attorneys to pay to smear the other party instead of allowing both parents to share the time equally.

This couldn't be further from the truth, as CYS found Karen's allegations unsubstantiated and closed the case on April 9th, 2018. When CYS called Ken to inform him of Karen's unfounded and unsubstantiated reports, he was really relieved. He had promised himself never to confess to a crime that he did not commit. He would fight for his rights until the end. Ken was determined to win because he wasn't doing this just for himself. He was doing it for his daughters too. He would not allow himself to be wrongfully thrown behind bars.

In Hon. Judge Carolyn T. Carluccio's own words in an interview:

"I will carry forward the practice I have always followed of fighting bias and discrimination, which is why I was chosen as a leader in the diversity committee. In my courtroom, everyone, regardless of race, class, gender, and ethnic background, will be treated fairly, professionally, and in accordance with the law."

If the Enforcement Officer had no "reasonable basis to find probable cause," why was Ken pursued and treated like a criminal? It seems his only crime was to expect fairness from a flawed system purposely built to split the justice system of this country.

This pattern shows up time and time again. It is strange how the same Judges who speak about fair treatment in their court do not mind harassing a black man despite there being no grounds to hold him.

You could say the system is fair, and the laws depict that, but the unfortunate truth is that on the ground, the reality is different. The papers and the pretentious smiling faces handling the law might claim that every courtroom goes through a fair trial. They could say there is no biasness in the system, but only hundreds and thousands of innocents who go through this pressure and unfairness can honestly tell you about justice. They will tell you about the nitty gritty and the grime that's hidden beneath the folds that the entire judiciary holds.

Ken stood his ground when he was accused of a hideous crime he hadn't committed. However, the same cannot be said for many people who succumb to the pressure. They realize they are not privileged enough to win this battle and choose to confess to crimes they did not commit.

Do you know how many people in America plead guilty in court when they are innocent? Why is that? What coerces them to give up and accept the retributions they don't deserve to go through? It is the realization that this is rigged and flowed to put the less privileged down and keep them under.

Ken couldn't imagine losing the precious time he should have been spending with his daughters. He would relentlessly fight for justice, no matter the roadblocks that would come his way. He knew it wouldn't be easy because he was too familiar with the justice system in the country. He knew about the bias against blacks and other minority groups but that would not deter Ken from seeking an acquittal. Just like Karen was doing everything she could to make up lies against him, he was doing everything he could to get himself out of this.

Every time Ken thought about this ordeal, he could hardly believe that they were the same couple who were happily married. Friends and family always admired them and thought of them as the perfect couple. They would enjoy different activities, go out for date nights, and visit their families.

Now, all that was long gone. The storm was here, and it was only getting worse. There was no hope of getting back to where they were before. Their beautiful love had faded away forever.

This realization became more evident to Ken when Karen came up with more lies on top of her false allegations. The incident happened when Ken called her to discuss CYS's outcome, upon which she insisted that the Abington police had not lifted the safety plan. This led Ken to believe that Abington Police and the District Attorney's Office of Montgomery County were prejudiced on having him wait before they closed their investigation on August 27th, 2018.

This was long after he underwent a polygraph exam on June 15th, 2018, which proved that he was not lying. Nonetheless, he and Karen entered into an Agreed Interim Order on April 18th, 2018, whereby they would share the legal custody, with Karen having the primary physical custody. Then a Court Order was issued on May 18th, stating that Ken would be allowed a weekly two-hour period of custodial time with the children to be supervised by the Assurance Group or another provider.

Subsequently, the custody conciliation was postponed until the resolution of the criminal investigation.

Ken had not seen his daughters between March till May 2018, when an order for supervised custody visitation was put into place. After Ken requested a protracted trial on May 15th, 2019, a final order was entered to allow him to see his kids unsupervised from June 1st till July 20th, 2019. Unfortunately, the deadbeat Judge, Carluccio, had entered an order to preposterously deter Ken's unsupervised visitation until July 30, 2019.

This only added to Ken's defamation. Later on, he and Karen appeared for a Custody Conciliation on February 28th, 2019. The two appeared before Master Sara Goren, who had made recommendations about his health and fitness to parent the girls and omitted her previous stance against his favorable PSE report that he "does not currently meet the DSM-V diagnostic criteria for any mental health disorders, including any sexual disorders."

Ken was compelled to believe that Judge Carluccio had shown an appearance of partiality ever since the Short List Conference for Custody on September 4th, 2018, because too few closed-door encounters in the chamber had been held with the opposing counsel, Ms. Song Chute. Ken's former counsel also shared with him that Hon. Judge Carluccio denied reimbursements for attorney fees of $10,000, as well as $3,000 for the cost of the court-ordered PSE exam when he consulted with him during a Hearing on April 25th, 2019.

According to Ken's attorney, Mr. Hamilton, Judge Carluccio's rationale was due to "frivolous filings" that she'd reason, bamboozle, and run the okey-dokey on all of his legal counsels. On the contrary, he allowed the opposing counsel, Ms. Chute, to make the argument about the so-called "bagged sheets." This proved that they chose to overlook the prejudice and be more determined than ever to discriminate in favor of Karen, despite Ken bringing the matter to the court's attention for both Support and Custody on January 22th and 24th, 2019. He elaborately highlighted how Karen stole his car. Still, nothing seemed to matter, not even her creating a toxic environment in their house or offering herself to "fuck, marry, or kill" random men on social media.

This Custody case was a matter of public importance for the public's good but Judge Carluccio had shown a stance of partiality and did not preserve Ken's rights and liberty based on facts. Rather, they saw the matter through the lens of conjecture, even when the case was not held with no arrest or a formal arraignment to follow.

It was clear that Judge Carluccio had established an unwarranted prima facie case ("on its face") for the opposing counsel, Ms. Chute, without any prosecution in a Custody matter, even though there was a favorable court-ordered PSE report. Not only had there been a violation of ethical principles or "Due Process" and Forgery (or "uttering a false instrument"), but suppression of evidence had also ensued following various motions for text transcripts and behavioral health records of Karen's malicious intent that she had displayed, by alleging that Ken sexually assaulted their oldest child.

According to the ATSA Code of Ethics, Section 3.02, the PSE exam that Judge Carluccio had ordered on October 23rd, 2018, per an attorney's request, was considered to be a violation of ethical principles due to the obvious limitations of assessments and their state-licensed health professionals (Fox & Maia, 2017).

Karen's false allegations led to mistreatment by the C.P. Montgomery County Court and Ms. Song Chute for having forged documents. This resulted in Karen's sole exclusive possession of their home and child support, which he could not afford despite obtaining employment in a company on June 3rd, 2019, after being unemployed since August 17th, 2018.

For Ken, it was devastating to realize that the

court not upholding the law only encouraged Karen and her attorney to purge the documents. Unfortunately, even after Karen was made aware that her allegations were baseless, she continued to press the custody case to her advantage. Eventually, this forced Ken to undergo a court-ordered psycho-sexual evaluation at his own expense against a "not arrested" entry in the system.

Ken was stung by charges of abuse of power and patronage by the C.P. Montgomery County Court, including Judge Carluccio's silence on the consideration for his acquittal, given mountains of evidence that exonerated him. Substantial evidence implicated that the opposing counsel and Karen – who had a history of mental health, compelled Ken to seek financial compensation for the attorney's fees and the cost of the evaluation, the sole physical custody, the sole legal custody of the two minor children, the sole exclusive possession of their home in Willow Grove, and for her to be psychologically evaluated for making false claims against him.

Chapter Eight: Petitions for Custody and Support in the Montgomery County Court of Common Pleas of Pennsylvania

In the course of these horrific outcomes, Ken filed for the custody and support of their daughters. He truly cared about their kids and didn't want marital issues to come between them. Whatever the outcome, Ken would always be there to protect and take care of them. He didn't want them to grow up without a father just because the parent's marriage didn't work out. He would dedicate his time to giving them all the love and protection they needed.

During the incident on March 10th, 2018, when Ken was at the Horsham Air National Guard base for the March Battle Assembly, he vented to a former business partner and friend, Nate, informing him about Karen's behavior around the house. He had also previously shared about Karen and her aunt's emotional outrage over little things to Nate.

I have always been inspired by the intricate yet strong feminine minds depicted in Jane Austen's novels. For instance, take her heroines from Northanger Abbey, Sense and Sensibility, or Pride and Prejudice. She had always made sure her heroines appeared to be more than kind-hearted, innocent, and beautiful creatures, from the period when the women's sole purpose was to socialize, get married, and raise children on an enormous estate while sipping tea with their pinkies out.

I admire how she subtly penned down the characters, making them feminists yet still staying far away as, ultimately, it always would boil down to marrying a man of high social caliber.

Her genius could not be doubted as she gave heroines from these now ancient periods thoughts and voices. In a time when little girls waited to come of age to marry and boys waited to become men and handle the business, her writing paved the way for a genre that separated gothic heroines.

If you look at the two characters from her novel Northanger Abbey, Isabella and Catherine, they are shown to be the total opposite of each other. While Isabella was upfront, bold and sharp-minded, Catherine was shy yet curious.

Karen often reminded Ken of Catherine's character. Her love of Gothic literature warped her reality and how she read people. Similarly, Karen also would feed from the gossip and opinions of her friends, which twisted her thoughts on feminism.

Catherine exhibited confusion in many moments and accidentally misled people because she lived in her fantasy world of Gothic literature and assumed people, in reality, portrayed themselves as who they were. This fascination of hers also led her to believe that the General had murdered his wife, which was far from the truth. In fact, Mrs. Tilney had died of natural causes. Catherine's views had been distorted toward reality, and it was a classic case of pseudo-feminism that led her to believe that it was a man who killed the woman. Throughout the novel, she listens to Isabella and absorbs her opinions and thoughts without wondering about her sudden engagement or other character whims.

She did not doubt her for a second, but the moment she read letters and received information that was out of context in the first place, she did not hesitate to form an opinion about the man who was an evident wrong-doer in her mind.

Karen's keen belief in her friends, who thought Ken was less of a feminist, is an evident piece of clue that joins these two characters.

Gothic literature has often portrayed that women who are abused and in distress are the ones who truly deserve a good man who will take care of them. Perhaps by falsely accusing Ken, Karen wanted to be the damsel in distress. Maybe it was a way to take the guilt away and make Ken the wrong person in this marriage. It is strange how mere thoughts inflicted and inspired by those around you can change the course of your life. Had Karen used her own thoughts and gotten the help she needed from professionals, perhaps the marriage wouldn't have been in the shambles it was now.

Her interest in Handmaid's Tale further aggravated her opinions and made her think of Ken in the wrong light. Perhaps the right help at the right time could have helped her, something her mother refused.

It is astonishing how a novel from the early 19th century portraying the society of the 18th century is still relevant in the 21st century when we are assumed to be trillions of miles ahead of that time.

Indeed, it is something to ponder over how pseudo-feminism still has a way of seeping into our society of civilized and educated people.

While the end of these Jane Austen novels is more accurate to the element where the heroines realize how wrong they were, you cannot deny that reality is far from the world Ms. Austen created when it comes to the round and meaningful endings.

If you think about it, Elizabeth Bennet's prejudice for Mr. Darcy was no less than a product of pseudo- feminism than Catherine's accusation of murder on General Tilney. Were the two men not made exemplary and refined villains by the women due to their views and opinions formed by the women and the resources around them?

Karen was quite similar in the way. She adopted her opinions and evaluations of society and, most importantly, Ken from her friends, who were in no way a better judge of his character.

At some point in their life, she had thought of Ken as the right person to be with. Perhaps that was one time when she disregarded her friend's opinion and saw Ken for who he really was. Or perhaps her friends approved at the time.

Whatever it was that changed could have been communicated in a better way. Unfortunately, her views were significantly affected. Her complaints about house chores and false claims about their sexual interaction were proof of what she wanted to portray to her friends. I firmly believe that had her mother taken things seriously and gotten her the help she needed instead of turning her back; the couple wouldn't have entered the particular space in the marriage that made Ken the crazy abusive man and Karen the damsel who had needed help all along. Although the latter stands true.

Feminism is essential to build this world up, but it is pseudo-feminism that is more relevant in today's society and has the power to deconstruct the good that feminism can bring into this world.

That said, by no means is patriarchy better. To me, it seems pseudo-feminism and patriarchy are two sides of the same coin. While one makes women think less of men, the other follows by putting women down because of their gender.

Catherine and Karen are both from different times, but their similar thought process goes to show what many men often have to go through.

Women are complex emotional creatures and are more prone to psychological problems than men due to their makeup. They have a much more complicated internal and emotional life than men. They live a large portion of their lives inside their thoughts. At the same time, men tend to live in a world of action outside of their heads. No, not all women are crazy. But they are usually much more complicated than men. And that's why men lose their patience and fail to learn the right way to handle women.

Every relationship requires communication. However, it is especially important for a couple. Without it, a couple can easily find themselves sliding down the path of a broken marriage. Two people who have vowed to be together forever will ultimately grow apart if they aren't honest with each other.

Relationships require work, and hiding your feelings does not do any good. Be aware that it doesn't just suddenly happen. It happens in short breaks, in tiny moments that we do not notice. The relationship slowly dies, and the couple grows apart as if the two ends of a magnet. Eventually, you start having more conflicts and lose the intimacy you both had.

This can happen when you depend too much on your partner for your happiness. It is essential to create your own path of happiness. Furthermore, it is also important to heal yourself and ask for help when needed. You must realize that your partner cannot read your mind. You must communicate your troubles and share your feelings about the relationship.

It is definitely not your partner's responsibility to deal with your emotional enigma. They can offer you support, but you cannot depend on them for your happiness. When you clearly share your thoughts and listen to each other, the relationship can blossom and become a safe space for both individuals.

Women are especially prone to depression after they have given birth, and if ignored, the depression can take over their entire life. It is essential for them to get help and be open about what they are going through. This is where their partner can offer them the right support and dedication to continue their relationship.

This is an excerpt from the National Association on Mental Illness (NAMI):

"1 in 8 women experience depression in their lifetime; twice the rate as men, regardless of their race or ethnic background. Nearly 18 million Americans experience depression every year. Some experiences are unique to women, including postpartum changes, infertility, and hormonal fluctuations throughout their lives."

Nate suggested that the best thing Ken ought to do was to go to the courthouse on the following Monday, March 12th, 2018, and file for both, Custody and Child Support. The divorce process would start soon afterward. Ken knew there was no coming back to such a marriage after the "foul shit like accusing a father of sexually abusing his own three year old daughter!" Ken did as Nate suggested and then served a copy in the mail for Karen to appear for the next court date next month, in April 2018.

Karen had always known Ken's half-brother, JP's run-ins with the law based on his false confessions for a lesser time as his attorney had him believe over two decades ago. JP had been living his life and raising his child with his then-girlfriend,

Mel, after his release from his sentence. He said that letting his attorney and the district attorney convince him to confess to a crime he did not commit, just so he'd get less time, was the biggest mistake of his life. This was a common practice in this country where many would wrongly confess to crimes they did not commit, leading to wrongful convictions being eventually overturned by DNA evidence that involved some form of a false confession.

In JP's case, he revealed that his attorney told him he would be better off getting lesser time in jail rather than spend the rest of his life imprisoned if he didn't admit to his jealous ex-girlfriend's accusations of having sexually abused her daughter.

Among the many arguments that came up was Karen's attorney Ms. Song Chute's series of onslaughts on making these outlandish arguments. She quoted the actions of JP's criminal past in court documents when the authorities found their allegations unfounded and unsubstantiated. The actions of Jeffery Dahmer definitely did not incriminate his family, who was a feared serial killer.

It occurred to Ken that Karen's primary goal was to make him and his family look as bad as possible. She wanted to paint the wrong picture of him, presumably so that she would be granted custody of the kids and so that he would be thrown in jail for an accusation that wasn't true. To even think that any of his family members could be made to feel like they were connected to a pedophile was heart-wrenching. There was no history of violence in their marriage. This made Ken wonder why in the world Karen had gone to such extreme lengths to falsely accuse him and do everything in her power to make him look like a criminal in the custody case. What's worse was that Judge Carluccio was conniving with her and her attorney in the courtroom.

Chapter Nine: Abington Police, The District Attorney (DA)'s Office of Montgomery County, Mission Kids, Opposing Counsel, and Mother

Ken reminded Karen of the unfounded report by the CYS. He knew she obviously wouldn't be happy to hear it, but he wanted to clarify that he would never confess to her false accusations. He also told her about the multiple opposing counsel calls. The next day, the detective called Ken and told him to go to the station for the "big picture."

However, this did not happen due to client-attorney privilege. Even with all the vetting Ken had been subjected to, he didn't change his original statement. He was innocent and was confident he would soon prove it. He got the impression that the Abington Police detective had been wasting police resources to immeasurably bolster Karen's allegations against him. After all her efforts to make him look bad, the authorities had no choice but to exonerate him of any wrongdoing.

As he thought about Karen's false allegations, Ken realized that they generally manifested little to no social taboos that were likely to come within the purview of women. Her behavior was different from anything he'd ever heard of. It was shocking as much as it was infuriating. Every night while Ken lay in bed, he tried to make sense of why Karen would make up such accusations against him. Every time, he couldn't find any justification for it. What mattered at the moment was to prove his innocence and fight for the custody of his kids.

The events that followed next were a clear indication that there was massive suppression of evidence. Ken wouldn't be wrong if he dubbed this experience as "one of the Greatest Witch Hunt in Family Law History." His unique situation involving Family Court suppressing evidence wasn't the first one. He learned that other parents had been subjected to similar mistreatments throughout the course of their custody and child support cases.

Since fathers were allowed to request medical records from the Children's Hospital of Philadelphia (CHOP), Ken made a request. He was able to review the records of both the girls. However, he was astounded to learn about the level of exposure and humiliation that the doctors and nurses had put his daughters through due to the standard procedure for abused victims.

The internal report of CYS on Karen's allegations being labeled UNFOUNDED should have been enough for the authorities to drop the case. Instead, they preposterously wasted Ken's time with their investigations. The Custody Conciliator tampered with the "foregone conclusion" that Mission Kids had secured and omitted the conclusion that favored Ken in the

Master's Report. Ken confided in his friend, Pierre, and told him about the difficult times he was going through.

"I'm also reluctant to participate in any future court proceedings since the courthouse and staff railroaded me. This led to the custody judge's orders being returned via mail to the courthouse," he said. "Yet, there is no process server banging on my door with a notice for the recusal as there is a new custody judge on the docket. It reflects that I am in violation of such a law for 'returning a letter to sender'."

Kanye West sang it best, "God isn't stopping these wars." So He's definitely not going to stop Ken when he returns the letter to the courthouse.

"This is one of the most disturbing cases I've heard about," Pierre said. "It's like they're trying to make it impossible so you can eventually give up. But don't do what they want. I know that you're innocent and I've got your back."

Later, you would learn that the VA tried to apportion Ken's VA benefits. Like the judicial actors, including private contractors going against the basic constitutional principles relevant to the enforcement of fines and fees. Still, Ken's response to the VA that mentioned that they violated the Social Security Act, among other laws, exuded no phone call or a knee-jerk write-back from them, except depositing his monthly check in the bank.

It should go without saying, but the VA's lackluster attempt to try and enforce apportionment of Ken's VA benefits was an example of unconstitutional practices by court staff and private contractors. Non-custodial parents (NCPs) have been seeing this for "nonpayment of fines and fees without first conducting an indigency determination and establishing that the failure to pay was willful" (DOD Letter). Eli Hager demonstrates this controversy in her article "Debtors' Prisons, Then and Now: FAQ," which rages today even after Congress outlawed debtors' prison and ruled it unconstitutional by the Supreme Court.

Non-custodial fathers are very easily stigmatized. It is horrifying that unless you fit into a box set by society, or, in this case, the American justice system, you can't have a character of your own.

Somehow it is deemed wrong to be right.

Take into consideration great men before us. Hasn't every man who tried to change perspective and the clichéd stereotypes of the world been subjected to this same stigma? Didn't Jesus get labeled as an extremist? As did Prophet Amos, who was called an extremist for justice. Let's not forget

Saint Paul, who was an extremist for the Christian gospel. Do non-custodial single fathers who comply with the law not align with such men?

While it is good to talk about fathers who certainly are deadbeat dads, it is astonishing that society doesn't want to speak about the noncustodial fathers who understand their responsibility and take it upon themselves to pay for child support and help through whatever is in their capacity.

Is it not time to break these stereotypes and stop judging every father that walks into the family court for a child custody case?

Perhaps noncustodial "upbeat" fathers should accept this judgment that befalls them since great men before them were just as easily stigmatized.

Obviously, that isn't a great solution.

It is quite disappointing to see family courts ignore the lessons we learn from history. The virtues displayed and the stigma they couldn't quite get away from should have been remembered to help us create a free society.

Since Ken's move to New York, he had stopped trusting the family Court of Montgomery County of Pennsylvania. In fact, he stopped engaging with them altogether until a recent development involving "Notice of Registration of Out-Of-State Support Order" per New York State's Article 5-B of the Family Court Act.

Congress keeps coming up with laws yet makes no attempts to analyze the possible interpretations and leaves that to administrative means.

I must share that these means are to a fault, especially the notice that required a response for a court hearing within 20 days. However, upon Ken's response, he'd then receive another mail for his response within 45 days, or he'd risk suspension of his driving privileges. That truly is the definition of what bureaucracy is because there's no due process!

Now non-custodial parents must pay child support, and if they fall into arrears or cannot pay due to any reason, such as unemployment, this pending payment is added to their credit reports.

At the same time, when a noncustodial parent applies for a job, they must undergo regular scrutiny and background check by the employer. Unfortunately, most employers will not hire potential employees with child support on their credit reports.

Even though this step is taken to encourage noncustodial parents to work and pay child support, the system does not work in their favor. In fact, it feels as if the system is made to make these parents fail.

Hence, noncustodial parents are forced to do off-the-table jobs (which do not pay much and are often below minimum wage) or build their own businesses (which can require a large sum of money).

Suppose Ken wanted to offer equity to a reputable equity firm to expand his business. Credit reporting would put all his plans for business at pause.

The Federal courts have recently issued rulings about using consumer reports to collect an account under the 2003 Fair Credit Reporting Act (FCRA) amendment.

Despite this, The Consumer Financial Protection Bureau (CFPB), a U.S. government agency whose purpose is to ensure that all banks, lenders, and other financial institutions treat every American fairly, has received multiple complaints. These complaints are regarding companies who ignore the rulings and do pre-employment checks, including the credit reporting of child support.

It is time for the Federal and American Justice system to take measures and work on fixing the broken child support program and work for the benefit of parents and children.

Ken was focused on holding on to his truth despite facing major setbacks. He wouldn't go down without a fight. Amid everything that was happening, the well-being of his daughters mattered the most. He had waited for nine months to hold them in his arms. Amazingly, their presence in his life brought a smile to his face in spite of the battle he was fighting. If he had no other reason to be strong, their existence was the one thing that would keep him from giving up.

You are only required to respond to the civil demand if you are served with a complaint and/or summons.

Following the violation, Karen's lawyer tried to file a petition for a lesser offense. However, the new judge denied her motion. The likelihood of having to sue the courthouse for discrimination and mishandling of both custody and child support was none. These judges had been abusing and taking advantage of the U.S. Constitution due to their judicial immunity. So unless something changed, this tyranny would continue to take its course. That being said, Ken believed that his case was, if not first, one of the many Family Court witch hunts in history.

Karen told Ken once that after five years into the marriage, she and Bob once shared some intimate moments right after she broke up with her undocumented-for ex-boyfriend, Antonio. What was going on in Karen's head after all these years that compelled her to share these intimate details about her supposed ex-boyfriend and friend? One would never know! Nevertheless, Ken felt disrespected and didn't take it lightly that Karen held a series of phone calls with Bob during his Annual Training in California, leading up to her allegations in March 2018.

Ken was starting to question just about everything in his marriage, especially Karen's motive, as she once shared a kiss with her best friend, whose marriage he attended. Tom and Jerry are the nicest gay couple anyone in the world would want to be friends with, regardless of their biases, religion, or creed.

Ken's thoughts were reflective of his Jewish ex-girlfriend, Andy, who once asked him during intimacy if he liked taking a dildo. This made Ken very uncomfortable, and he ended up bursting out of the room and slamming the doors on her. However, he did apologize to her the next day. She was in no position to try and figure out what to pull out first if Ken were to stick a knife in her back and a finger in her butt. That's like comparing a dick with a finger.

It begs the question of whether Tom was ever elated when Kathy Perry sang "I Kissed a Girl" and how she liked it. Ken used to think that he would never want a close gay friend who would put quaalude in his drink, only to find out the next morning that his butt hurt as if he'd been with Jeffrey Dahmer. He thought this way because of Cardi B's confession about drugging and robbing men in their homes.

However, only insecure people with deep-rooted fear and revulsion refuse to change their attitude about gay men. This waste of energy goes a long way with Kevin Samuels, who once cleared up the controversy about a leaked viral clip of a man found sleeping in his bed when he accidentally pressed the wrong button during a live stream. As it turned out, the man was a troll queued to purposely gay-bash straight men. At the same time, the LGBTQ community stood idly as his critics hurled out homophobic slurs. You'd best believe that to have been a smear in order to damage his reputation.

Everything was turning out to be more dramatic than ever. First, Ken learned that Karen stole and sold his 2010 Toyota Corolla. This happened when he went to Warsaw in December 2018. Karen paid a visit to Ken's old Philly apartment, took his car, and claimed to have sold it. The authorities investigated and apparently believed only what she had told them. Later on, an Abington Police detective revealed that Karen, Lizzie, and her husband were at their home during the time when this incident was reported, and Karen was on a call with him.

After Karen's accusations and the ongoing investigation in their home after CPS's request, Ken discovered two condoms in the master bedroom. One of them read: "Make Me Cum!"

Later on, Ken became friends with their neighborhood friend, Lilly Howard's ex-husband, Maxwell, who told Ken that Karen showed Lilly that set of condoms with a smile on her face. Ken confronted Karen about it.

"What's the meaning of this?" Ken demanded, showing them to Karen. Karen was surprised and speechless, as she didn't see it coming. She was ashamed and chose not to answer him. Soon afterward, she ended her friendship with Lilly. Maxwell later showed Ken some of Karen's pictures on the Ok! Cupid dating app. Karen's other social media accounts were also very provocative and were for soliciting random men to the same house while Family Court was protecting her.

Karen's profile read "Game of Thrones Edition: Marry, Fuck, and Kill!" Upon seeing this, Ken felt her intentions were not good right from the moment they met. He felt like he didn't know Karen at all. She was a completely different person as compared to the woman Ken had fallen in love with. Karen even tried to make his daughters believe he didn't care about them. It was so hurtful because it was the opposite of what he felt. He deeply cared about them and would do anything to ensure they were safe and comfortable.

The lies being made up and spread around about Ken were devastating. He longed for the day when this battle would be over. Although he knew that he still had a long way to go since the so-called "justice" system seemed to be working against him. The same system that should have defended him was making his life a living hell. He resorted to tapping into his inner strength so that he could get through these tough days.

The way that the C.P. Montgomery County discriminated against Ken shows how Americans should be terrified of their judicial system, as this could happen to anyone. Even if you're not guilty, evidence can be tampered with to convict you. You might even be forced to admit to a crime you didn't commit!

As a law-abiding country, I believe that you cannot allow someone to conduct themselves as if the law doesn't apply to them. Whether someone is a judge, an attorney, or a detective, they should be treated equally under the law. The sad thing is that these judges had devalued the importance of custody and support as "immunity" to protect themselves from lawsuits. There has even been an incident of a judge ordering a house search without a warrant. When the victim tried to protest, they were forcefully silenced and threatened. This is a perfect example of abuse of power because they know there is nothing that the victims can do.

In his case, Ken faced an uphill battle to get the girls because the judges did nothing in his favor due to Karen's white race. They also knew Ken hated her guts after what she had done to him.

Although the kids were young with serious allergies, the judges at the courthouse engaged in some sort of witch hunt with their onslaught of discrimination. Ken knew he needed to press the judge for a trial back in June 2019, as he didn't trust her judgment. Karen's lawyer made up lies that the judge listened to without raising any questions. Next up was an order for supervision, which he refused because the allegations were biased and wrong, and he didn't want to put up with it.

Going through a custody battle was like going through a war where one does not emerge unscathed by a recused judge. However, he learned important lessons as he was left broken and incapable of trusting Judge Carluccio, or any other judge for that matter. He had lost faith in the so-called justice system,

In the diagram below, you can see that Judge Carluccio made the court decision beyond the "not arrested" entry into the system. The diagram shows specific steps that are required in the administration of criminal justice based on the U.S. Constitution to safeguard one's individual freedom against unlawful measures from law enforcement agencies.

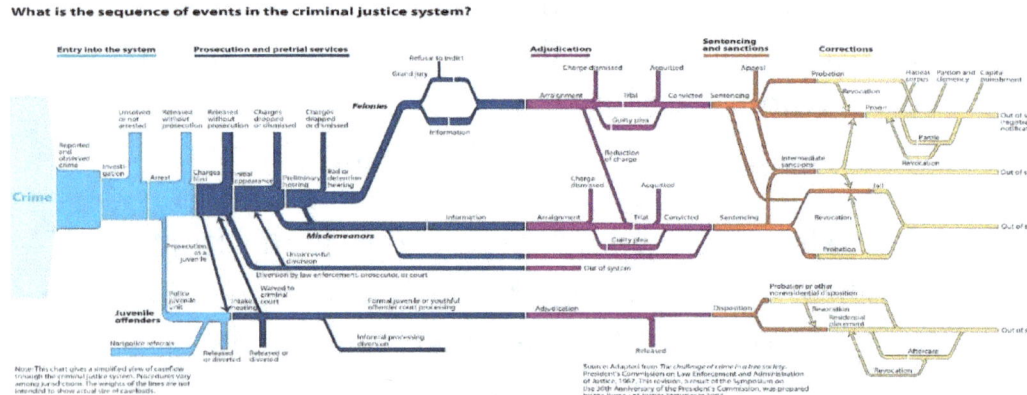

("Criminal Justice System Flowchart," 2021).

The injustice carried out by these judges at the C.P. Montgomery County Court equates to historical turncoat moments. Similar to those of Lincoln's successor, Andrew Johnson, who rescinded the "40 acres and a mule" policy to the nation's estimated 3.9 million former slaves in the fall of 1865 (Gates, 2013).

Since Andrew Johnson's rejection of the Civil Rights Act of 1866, which was overridden by

Congress, President Woodrow Wilson practiced racist policymaking of resegregation. He insisted on placing Black federal workers in literal cages built around their workstations~~work stations~~ to "separate" those who could not work with their white colleagues ["The Federal Government and Negro Workers under President Woodrow Wilson (n.d.)."].

Another racist policy of resegregation was made by President Grant, who took the extreme measure of suspending the writ of habeas corpus in South Carolina to combat efforts to deprive black people of the right to vote. This was fully in accord with Mr. Stevenson when he says in his documentary, "True Justice: Bryan Stevenson's Fight for Equality," that it rested on the racist notion that blacks were treated less than humans and were always left to hold the shorter end of the stick due to discrimination based on their race. Ken could really relate to this, as the court treated him unfairly based on his race and gender.

Now it is important to note that prejudice is not only based on racist policies or behavior. In fact, it is also the political ideologies and theories that back it. This goes back to the Progressive era when scientific management principles were used to "regulate the American economy." NCPs should be aware of these historical agendas that still grip the folds of American society.

To understand today's political stance, it is essential to go back in time and analyze the Progressive era when society was transforming, and America was recovering from a civil war.

While many people dote about the fact that the Progressive Era of Woodrow Wilson brought about change in American society, the policies, and plans for altering the Declaration of Independence, the discriminatory policies introduced for immigrants, and the clear intention of supporting the idea of "survival of the fittest" states otherwise. This is also why he praised the British system of government.

It is surreal that policymakers rejected the central thought and the major preface of the Constitution that all people are equal and deserve every right. The people form the government and then bow down to their policies in acceptance. The state only exists because of the people. Despite their boosted egos, it is not the other way around.

Ken had a judge trying to make him pay for child support, although he was no longer in the army. There was simply no way out of it because of the judicial immunity that the court had. Victims of this mistreatment are usually powerless, and because standing up for their rights has been made the hardest thing to do, they often end up giving in to court orders. Many of them suffer long-term mental health issues, including depression and anxiety, because of the turmoil they have to endure during such harrowing cases.

There are organizations that offer support to parents who are going through or have gone through a similar experience as Ken, including [Dad Talk Today](), [The Child Support & Fatherless Crisis Hustle](), [The Father's Rights Movement](), [DAD - Dads Assisting Dads](), [Patriots for Parents Equality](), [Equal Justice Initiative](), [National Responsible Fatherhood Clearinghouse (NRFC)](), and [Meek Mill's Reform Alliance]().

These organizations are against the flawed court system. They advocate for 50/50 split parenting, something that is aimed at eradicating the kind of modern-day slavery that doesn't favor noncustodial parents ["I Stand with John (Full Documentary)," 2021]. Many, including Meek Mill, the music mogul, and rapper who was jilted at the altar by Judge Genece Brinkley after she sentenced him to two to four years for a parole breach - even though prosecutors asked for no prison time (Mill, 2021), would agree that "no one should be locked up for visiting a loved one, going to a family BBQ, picking up their kids, missing a meeting, or for being broke" ("Reform Alliance," 2021).

The United States Department of Justice "recently released a detailed letter outlining the injustices that the Department of Justice (DOJ) has committed against the financially less fortunate citizens of the United States." Before any arrest is made, government officials must follow for such warrants and arrests to be legal and constitutional. "As proven in many child support cases that have ended in arrests, most people detained are not criminals… they are just poor."

According to the Letter, courts must not incarcerate a person for nonpayment of fees without conducting an indigency determination. Moreover, courts must not use arrest warrants or license suspensions as a means of coercing the payment of court debt when individuals have not been afforded constitutionally adequate procedural protections. Those affected must be granted their constitutional rights and protection during the process for the violations that occur when a defendant is in contempt of court" (The DOJ Letter and Child Support Enforcement, 2021).

Family Courts across the country forget that the U.S. Constitution is limited to certain enumerated ends while justice is the cornerstone of government and civil society. The Deadbeat Judge made numerous wrong decisions as they were the product of invalid court proceedings that flagrantly denied Ken's due process rights.

Family Courts routinely deprive people of their civil rights under the "color of law," which represents a government official or somebody acting under the government's authority. The onset of the New Deal instituted by President Franklin D. Roosevelt during the Great Depression aimed to restore prosperity to Americans through a series of programs and projects.

Since then, we have seen lobbyists shove their administrative laws down our throats and involve the Supreme Court in ruling that "corporations are people." This dramatically expanded the corporate rights for which they aren't mentioned in the U.S. Constitution. It goes to show that the American government today is much different from the constitutional republic outlined in The Federalist Papers — which relies on structure, representation, and limitations on the functions of the federal government.

Administrative regulations and entitlements are two distinguishing features of modern government. These new features require a type of government that is unlimited, disregards the separation of powers, and violates the supreme law under which it claims to operate. Unless Congress restores the Separation of Powers doctrine guaranteed under the US Constitution, we'll continue to allow Administrative Law Judges to spray vitriol on non-custodial parents.

Family Court judges who fail to punish

malicious slander or libel against other people are going against the constitution. Don't just take my word for it. Benjamin Franklin had reason to believe there's no point in having a civil society if the government doesn't stop someone from destroying your reputation based on malicious claims.

In other words, the only way people can vindicate themselves is to hide out in a dark alley and wait for their accuser to come by and sucker-punch them senseless. You would think that's delusional. Yet, Machiavelli believed that to institute a republic is to presuppose that all men are wicked. This means to say that the majority of the people today are "industrious and uninformed."

Franklin further discussed the strength of media and how it has the power to change beliefs and narratives. The press, even today, has the ability to mold the public's perception. Benjamin Franklin emphasizes this in his short essay "An Account of the Supremest Court of Judicature in Pennsylvania, viz., The Court of the Press." He believes that the press holds more power than the judiciary since it has no laws and can malign any person's image without any consequences because they don't have rules to abide by. He even used humor to drive the point that the press should be free to print whatever they want as long as man is free to break the head of the person who has made malicious claims on someone's character.

While the free press is a good concept, it does need accountability, and a line must be drawn to indicate how far the press has gone. Franklin argued for the libel law to protect reputation. Benjamin Franklin famously said,

"Those who would give up essential Liberty, to purchase a little temporary Safety, deserve neither Liberty nor Safety."

You may understand this quote better by this instance that we give up some nonessential liberty for long-term safety when we give the state the right to search our properties with a warrant. This guarantees safety to participate in a society where some people are deemed criminal due to involvement in certain activities, which are also defined by the state. We willingly give up this liberty to ensure our long-term safety since this is more important despite the fact that it takes away some of our freedom. If you think about it, liberty in its entirety will only cause tyranny. This would put the state and the people constantly at war. This could be similar to how people rise up to get essential liberty against the state when they know they are giving up safety temporarily.

Benjamin Franklin repeated these words during the time of the Revolution in Santo

Domingo. Now, it is essential to bring your attention to the Revolutionary War of the 18th century, when enslaved people in Santo Domingo raised their voices against the Spanish and decided to take back their freedom. Slavery in itself is an astonishing aspect of colonization. The residents are made to bow down to the people who have taken over their land and all resources because they appear to be less than the "supreme whites." Slavery and Spanish colonization are a dark part of American history that shaped much of our society today. Although this happened in South America, it also affected our society. The French brought "slaves" from different colonies to America. When the enslaved people revolted and a war that lasted a decade began, it scared the likes of Jefferson, who feared that an independent Black nation could be its economic rival. Many white Americans were fearful of the idea. They believed that Haiti could not hold governance, much less maintain an entire nation, because white people couldn't understand the purpose of their revolt. These people were afraid that the revolution would spread to the United States and so abolished any means of connecting economically or politically with Haiti to ensure the radical ideas did not make their way to the U.S.

Jefferson's actions played a big part in crippling Haiti's economy, which he used to form the narrative that this happened because of African incompetence in governing. He never owned the fact that this was a cause of using all resources to cut ties and isolate Haiti to ever move towards progress. It is essential to remember that it was John Adams who initially helped Toussaint-Louverture in their cause. Of course, it was a political alliance that favored both parties, and this further cemented Franklin's thoughts on liberty.

However, Hamilton played a big part when Haiti was drafting its constitution and advised on its drafting. He encouraged open trade with them, and Jefferson was horrified at the very thought of this exchange with "a black nation."

Afterward, slave-holding communities were terrified because they expected the black communities in the United States to initiate a revolt. After all, such "radical ideas of equality" could also have spread here.

I'm a thinking man, and I believe in even allowing a small fraction of thought and belief that's safe over the majority of factions. Because man compares himself with others by his capacity for speech and reason, self-government is the rule of reason over passion.

There appears to be no solution in law against this abuse, even though Supreme Court Justice John Roberts once said, "the way to stop discrimination on the basis of race is to stop discriminating on the basis of race."

When you have judges, court staff, and attorneys work together — there are too many cooks spoiling the broth. These "psychological gymnastics" continue to manifest themselves to this day in our altered world, the idea of which stems from the World Economic Forum (WEF) founder and executive chairman Klaus Schwab's book COVID-19: The Great Reset.

He writes that the COVID-19 crisis should be regarded as an "opportunity that can be seized to make the kind of institutional changes and policy choices that will put economies on the path towards a fairer, greener future." Whether you know what the Great Reset is or not, this long-held belief of an established new normal, which is not a conspiracy theory, shows that the pandemic crisis has provided a pretext for finally enacting it "in terms of the convergence of economic, monetary, technological, medical, genomic, environmental, military, and governance systems."

It is evident that under this guise, Mr. Schwab wishes to form a tyrannical government that will rule the entire world. Can you muster to imagine the power they will hold? The Great Reset displays many good virtues when you first see it, but the deeper you examine the cause and the clause, you will clearly see the horrors depicted in the text.

Such radical ideas must be shut down. This will clearly set us back, and power will once again be used to fulfill the needs of the elite while the few rights that the public do have will be snatched from them. The "one-world order," as it used to be referred to, has been amended and made to look like it is in favor of the public. It is quite the opposite.

However, Article 5 and a call for a Convention of States can eliminate absurd ideas much like those proposed by Klaus Schwab. The right bestowed upon the public and states is a powerful one that the elite and higher authorities have long tried to disregard.

While people like Mr. Schwab push for The Great Reset, people want to limit the power national governments hold over the people and the states, and rightly so. Article 5 gives the people power to hold a Convention of the States and make amendments to the Constitution to put restraints on the Federal Government and stop a tyrannical government from working in its own favor despite the fact that they come in the position to govern for the people.

These bureaucrats~~beaurocrats~~ are in office for the people yet oppose their constitutional right to call a convention and make amendments that will be best for the nation as a whole. The elite and people in power continuously push propaganda against Article 5, calling it a "dangerous path that puts all our rights, civil liberties, and freedom at risk." This is far from the truth, as anyone who has studied Article 5 and the process of calling a convention would understand.

Such people take advantage of the public's naiveness and lack of knowledge to scare the citizens and make them believe in the myths of "runaway conventions."

The states have fully displayed the amendments they mean to focus on. The agenda is to:

- Impose fiscal restraints on Federal Government

- Limit their power and jurisdiction

- Impose term limits on Federal officials (members of Congress and Judiciary)

The purpose is to limit the power of Washington DC wrongfully used to accomplish things that are not in the public's best interest. These politicians and so-called Congressmen only display these stunts of excessive spending and power to return to the podium. It ensures that they maintain control and nothing, and no one in their midst can be held accountable for it.

The passing of amendments will ensure that the national office works for the people instead of against them, and decisions will be made to make the life of citizens easier rather than increasing their chances of maintaining power.

Furthermore, limiting terms will ensure that new people and ideas who represent the people equally will govern the office to make way for a better society.

Derrick Bell, one of the founders of critical race theory, argued in 1991 that black people had made no progress in the United States since 1865. Moreover, even Ta-Nehisi Coates came up with the precisely same conclusion: "White supremacy is a force so fundamental to America that it is difficult to imagine the country without it.

You are often told that "it only takes one person to make a change." This is nothing but a myth. Perhaps one person can make a change, but not the kind of change that would raise your status to be equal to your countrymen."

It is astonishing how the human mind can form a perception about someone with very little information. We could say that it is natural, and with time, as a person evolves, they learn to put aside the prejudice that is built in from childhood and the experiences we gain from society.

That said, the reality is different. Society as a whole still holds power over us, and it is hard to stand against something the whole world agrees on. Humans like to mirror everything. They wish to belong and act in unison. Anybody who stands up against this system is shut down.

Look at how the world was divided into black and white, rich and poor. It was considered the way of life, and those at the fairer end of the stick never questioned it.

When people started to protest and utter a few words about the atrocities, they were labeled enemies and traitors to the system. Indeed, it was preposterous, to say the least.

Similarly, the media holds a lot of power to change perceptions and portray certain people how the elite or the "controlling powers" of the world want us to perceive these people.

This is not even difficult to illustrate. Simply take Martin Luther King, who was labeled as an extremist. Why? Because he went against the tide. His refusal to back down and his continued call to action against the powerful made him an easy yet stubborn target. The man went through thick and thin to stand for the civil rights of every black man, woman, and child. All he asked for was fair treatment. Yet he was treated as a terrorist.

Even though this happened decades ago and he succeeded in bringing the change from the movement, somehow, society (or rather some of it) still refuses to change and accept people for who they are. The fact that our justice system, to this date, doesn't see why people of color need fair trials and representation is proof of that.

The civil rights lawyer Ben Crump portrays this well in his Netflix documentary Civil: Ben Crump. He states that the American justice system is clearly divided into black and white. He further stated:

"Symbols matter. Images matter. It is so powerful for history that we protect images that unite people that are multicultural, multiracial, multi-geographical, what is the direct opposite of that statue there... of that Confederate general. It is that image that is an affront to the Declaration of Independence."

This resonated with the thoughts presented by Frederick Douglass. The words spoken by Ben Crump don't solely boost the American Blacks, but it elevates the derivative Mr. Douglass held. For him, promoting race pride was similar to what the nonwhite people in America have been against since the beginning.

Firstly it is essential to humanize every person since the first banner we all stand under is that of a human. With that said, does every human not deserve to have similar rights without analyzing distinctions? He believed that every right a white American had should be freely granted to all people of color.

However, we still seem to be stuck in the same dilemma that has been a part of the system since the beginning of American history.

How could you say we have moved on from this racial injustice and discrimination if Ben Crump had to stand and talk about a Black America and a White America during a Black Lives Matter rally in the 21st century? How is it any different from Martin Luther King speaking about the rights of a Black person in the civil right movement way back in the 1960s?

Now, how could you say that Ken, who was a black man, got a chance at a fair trial, and every party involved in the case's judiciary process did not jump to the conclusion that he was a deadbeat dad because a white woman said so? Let me add, despite there being no significant evidence!

This surreal stereotype of fathers being deadbeats is another superficial perception that is a part of our society. No one ever questions how true or relevant it is in today's world.

Both Ken and Karen can take a break from simply bashing each other and recognize that, at times, Family Court can deal you a bad hand in many different ways. In this case, it was due to the hasty and monumental errors of a Deadbeat Judge. However, they should also realize that it is on them to learn from this ordeal and fix it.

Despite Ken's emotional and financial turmoil due to the gravity of this case, he still finds the strength to wake up with a positive outlook each morning, knowing that his daughters need him to be there for them and provide for them. Although Ken may be separated from Karen, he feels he needs to be as amiable as one can be with her for their sake. He will continue putting his differences aside to facilitate a safe environment where they can easily co-parent. And he hopes that Karen will continue doing the same, provided that he has the magnanimity to forgive her for everything she did.

END

Bibliography

"Women & Depression. 1 in 8; twice the rate of men." The National Association on Mental Illness (NAMI), April 28, 2008. https://www.nami.org/Press-Media/Press-Releases/2008/Women-Depression-1-in-8;-twice-the-rate-of-men

"Criminal Justice System Flowchart." Bureau of Justice Statistics, 3 June 2021, https://bjs.ojp.gov/media/image/45506.

"Deadbeat Judge." Facebook, https://www.facebook.com/deadbeatjudge.

"The DOJ Letter and Child Support Enforcement." The Child Support Hustle®, 6 Dec. 2021, https://thechildsupporthustle.com/2020/07/28/the-doj-letter-and-child-support-enforcement/amp/.

"The Federal Government and Negro Workers under President Woodrow Wilson (n.d.)." United States Department of Labor, https://www.dol.gov/general/aboutdol/history/shfgpr00.

Fox, Erik, and Maia Christopher. "ATSA 2017 Code of Ethics." ATSA, 2017, https://www.atsa.com/Public/Ethics/ATSA_2017_Code_of_Ethics.pdf.

Carey, Gideon W., and McClellan, James. "The Federalist: The Gideon Edition." Liberty Fund, Inc., 2001.

Gates, Henry Louis. "The Truth behind '40 Acres and a

Mule'." The Root, 7 Jan. 2013,
https://www.theroot.com/the-truth-behind-40-acres-and-a-mule-1790894780.

"I Stand with John (Full Documentary)." YouTube, 3 Oct. 2021, https://youtu.be/H_z0AfxT2bE. Accessed 23 Jan. 2022.

Stevensons, Bryan. "True Justice: Bryan Stevenson's Fight for Equality." HBO, 10 June 2019,
https://www.hbo.com/documentaries/true-justice-bryan-stevensons-fight-for-equality.

"Reform Alliance." REFORM Alliance, 2 Dec. 2021,
https://reformalliance.com/.

Mill, Meek. "Free Meek." Amazon Prime Video, 2019,
https://www.amazon.com/Free-Meek-Season-1/dp/B0875TQ2LB.

"International Fpies Association (I-FPIES) Home."
International FPIES Association, 23 May 2021,
https://www.fpies.org/.

Totenberg, Nina. "When Did Companies Become People? Excavating The Legal Evolution." NPR, July 28, 2014.
https://www.npr.org/2014/07/28/335288388/when-did-companies-become-people-excavating-the-legal-evolution

Mitchell, Will. "Kansas Senate passes shared parenting 39 to 1." CJOnline, Feb 9, 2020.
https://www.pratttribune.com/story/opinion/columns/20

20/02/09/will-mitchell-kansas-senate-passes-shared-parenting-39-to-1/112026552/

Duncan-Smith, Nicole. "Black Man Wrongfully Convicted In 1981 Rape of Now-Famous Author Alice Sebold Sues State of New York for $50 Million." Atlanta Black Star, March 1, 2022. https://atlantablackstar.com/2022/03/01/black-man-wrongfully-convicted-of-1982-rape-of-now-famous-author-alice-sebold-sues-state-of-new-york-for-50-million/?utm_source=facebook&utm_medium=news_tab

Roberts, Nigel. "Supreme Court Declines To Review Decision That Freed Bill Cosby From Prison: The comedian and actor served more than two years of a three-to-10-year sentence." BET, March 7, 2022. https://www.bet.com/article/0knhly/supreme-court-declines-review-bill-cosby-sexual-assault-case?utm_source=facebook&utm_medium=news_tab

Fox, Megan. "31 Missouri Judges Recuse Themselves from Lawsuit Alleging Family Court Guardians and Psychologists Orchestrated Money-Making Scheme" PJ Media, Mar 02, 2021.

https://pjmedia.com/news-and-politics/megan-fox/2021/03/02/31-missouri-judges-recuse-themselves-from-lawsuit-alleging-family-court-guardians-and-psychologists-orchestrated-money-making-scheme-n1428930?fbclid=IwAR3WELwuOZOeT-N3_SqWZ9xu-YVsPJI53ZpAmnoJPMutF4d3J0UvwId2lzA

Pierson, Lacie. "W.VA.'s 50-50 custody law now in effect." HD, Jun 11, 2022. https://www.herald-dispatch.com/news/w-va-s-50-50-custody-law-now-in-effect/article_02b6cf4d-80e5-5f0d-b348-e3c24480cf98.html?fbclid=IwAR1-X8_GDfIN8pHxw9_zsmn2JBr87SX8sB2WiD_QIBA2KwZ9_vC1JKkj5HM

Rothstein, Richard. "The Color of Law: A Forgotten History of How Our Government Segregated America." Liveright, 2017. https://www.lisc.org/media/filer_public/df/b8/dfb840c9-83da-454c-bcf8-d1844b04d049/color-of-law-summary_handout.pdf

Nischalke, Rick. "Corrupt Family Court System and apathy are destroying our nation." Parental Alienation - Keeping Families Connected Blog, July 6, 2010.

https://www.keepingfamiliesconnected.org/blog/corrupt-family-court-system-and-apathy-are-destroying-the-our-nation

Bikales, James. "After 91 years, Black teen exonerated by a defense lawyer's great-grandson." The Washington Post, June 18, 2022.

https://www.washingtonpost.com/history/2022/06/18/pennsylvania-teen-exonerated/?utm_source=facebook&utm_medium=news_tab&fb_news_token=rgxzdZpt9rv%2FHtYTAGF8hQ%3D%3D.KqjQbPKNrY0xSLRfLxfE4TgT0%2BnlqsUvTcI1tFV3H%2FfzUm2Jw7oqVHiEt1IsRdLNNaZtxCmBhnav3B7mduoLWmnztsPpk44zZA1TDGhq4a5jCC

CMxjDRSb2ca8488ZEGAWMG7gpMXEi1UnPA1o6R
OcACT0e6CIlsjg1ceD7MMGGsZxGoFK8WJKEIu9Ey
r2yPg0vKGzGNUqzCuLTWFTFmEa9PbfkbeNoyy1zZ
tt8HYcCORJB%2FSKKRV7JXAQCLZFP%2B9GXRt
%2BqHWkFgD8a8f2Ul0%2B0DivaW%2BRdiJQB506
GJ9jgFOVviEPhFEsv79ugh6Qnr

Blotcky, Alan D. "The Weaponization of False Allegations of Abuse." Psychiatric Times. July 26, 2022.

https://www.psychiatrictimes.com/view/the-weaponization-of-false-allegations-of-abuse

Robertson, Robbie. "City Of Stillwater Oklahoma Mayor And City Manager Involved In Second Lawsuit." The Oklahoma Post, July 29.

https://theokpost.com/complimentary-content/oklahoma-politics-news/city-of-stillwater-oklahoma-mayor-and-city-manager-involved-in-second-lawsuit?fbclid=IwAR17cJHdfWel1i7XykmfaLWtfzys8j9IH-YPZCP__Ihu55t_IZq8l9cS6CY

Hager, Eli. "Debtors' Prisons, Then and Now: FAQ - Congress outlawed them. The Supreme Court ruled them unconstitutional. Yet they live on." Justice.Gov - USAO-SDL, February 24, 2015.

https://www.justice.gov/usao-sdal/page/file/918356/download

Lepore, Jill. "I.O.U.: How we used to treat debtors."

Annals of Finance, April 6, 2009.
https://www.newyorker.com/magazine/2009/04/13/i-o-u

Rectenwald, Michael. "What Is the Great Reset? Part I:
Reduced Expectations and Bio-techno-feudalism."
Michael Rectenwald, December 16, 2020.
https://www.michaelrectenwald.com/great-reset-essays-interviews/great-reset-part-1-reduced-expectations-gly6a?rq=Great%20reset

Miles, ByDarla. "Court docs: Missing NJ girl was
beaten to death, mom kept collecting child support: The
family of the suspect, Matthew Chiles III, spoke
exclusively to Eyewitness News." Eyewitness News,
August 9, 2022. https://abc7ny.com/missing-child-welfare-check-mothers-boyfriend-murder-charge/12111945/?fbclid=IwAR0CdFYXRvdijNQHfVl
kbVyg7NEkO8N5o_8dKwjO0Kuc12rPsXSRJgUcPBc#
l6nn8b7x69qbv6vn6o6

Lister, Nolan. "Helena man accused of shooting threat
over child support payments." Independent Records,
Aug 23, 2022. https://helenair.com/helena-man-accused-of-shooting-threat-over-child-support-payments/article_96e08ce3-07b5-548e-853b-5d5f0492316e.html

Feulner, Edwin J. "The right way to think about rights."
The Heritage Foundation, Aug 27th, 2013.
https://www.heritage.org/political-process/commentary/the-right-way-think-about-rights

Tray, Morgan. "Cleveland judge accused of more than

100 counts of misconduct blames menopause, sleep apnea." ABC 5, April 12. 2022.

https://www.news5cleveland.com/news/local-news/cleveland-metro/cleveland-judge-accused-of-more-than-100-counts-of-misconduct-blames-menopause-sleep-apnea?fbclid=IwAR2MHP6lyUYvlH_B1IQUVlUBVdJnY9Hn6rg0W59xxTJYJuXzv24ZeAggH3Q

Hessler Jr, Carl. "Judge Carolyn Tornetta Carliccio to lead Montgomery County bench as next president judge." The Mercury, November 5, 2021.

https://www.pottsmerc.com/2021/11/05/judge-carolyn-tornetta-carluccio-to-lead-montgomery-county-bench-as-next-president-judge/amp/

Judge Carolyn Carluccio. Main Line Today Staff, 2014. Retrieved from https://mainlinetoday.com/uncategorized/judge-carolyn-carluccio/amp/

Inquirer Judicial Candidate Questionnaire. (n.d.). Retrieved from http://media.philly.com/documents/carlucci_montco.pdf

Hessler Jr, Carl. "Montgomery County bench welcomes two new judges." Times Herald, January 16, 2018. https://www.timesherald.com/2018/01/16/montgomery-county-bench-welcomes-two-new-judges/amp/

Fair Credit Reporting. (n.d.). Retrieved from

https://www.federalreserve.gov/boarddocs/supmanual/cch/200906/fcra.pdf
TITLE 15—COMMERCE AND TRADE. (n.d.). Retrieved from https://www.govinfo.gov/content/pkg/USCODE-2011-title15/pdf/USCODE-2011-title15-chap41-subchapIII-sec1681b.pdf

CONGRESSIONAL RECORD — Extensions of Remarks. (1995, January 5). Retrieved from https://www.govinfo.gov/content/pkg/CREC-1995-01-05/pdf/CREC-1995-01-05-pt1-PgE43.pdf

Matthews, Allie Page. "Credit Reporting Agencies." Office of the Child Support Enforcement: An Office of the Administration for Children & Families, May 24, 1990. Retrieved from https://www.acf.hhs.gov/css/policy-guidance/credit-reporting-agencies

Child Support Enforcement Legislative History. (n.d.). Retrieved from https://greenbook-waysandmeans.house.gov/2012-green-book/child-support-enforcement-cover-page/legislative-history

Child Support Enforcement. The United States Department of Justice, May 28, 2020. Retrieved from https://www.justice.gov/criminal-ceos/child-support-enforcement
CITIZEN'S GUIDE TO U.S. FEDERAL LAW ON CHILD SUPPORT ENFORCEMENT. The United

States Department of Justice, May 28, 2020. Retrieved from
https://www.justice.gov/criminal-ceos/citizens-guide-us-federal-law-child-support-enforcement

Nischalke, Rick. "Corrupt Family Court System and apathy are destroying our nation." Parental Alienation-Keeping Families Connected Blog, July 16, 2010. https://www.keepingfamiliesconnected.org/blog/corrupt-family-court-system-and-apathy-are-destroying-the-our-nation

Austen, Jane (Author), Fraiman, Susan (Editor). Northanger Abbey. Norton Critical Editions, October 6, 2004.

Austen, Jane (Author), Johnson, Claudia L (Editor). Jane Austen: Sense and Sensibility. Norton Critical Editions, October 30, 2001.

Austen, Jane (Author), Gray, Donald (Editor), Favret, Mary A (Editor). Pride and Prejudice. Fourth Norton Critical Editions, June 1, 2016.

Arnn, Larry P. Churchill's Trial: Winston Churchill And The Salvation Of Free Government. Nelson Books, 2015.

Hanson, Victor Davis. The Dying Citizen: How Progressive Elites, Tribalism, and Globalization Are Destroying the Idea of America. Basic Books, October 5, 2021

Aristotle (Author), Sachs, Joe (Translator).

Nicomachean Ethics. Focus Philosophy Library, 2021.

Hamadeh, Yasmeen. "The details of the 'The Jeffrey Dahmer Story' trailer are too disturbing for a headline." Mashable, September 16, 2022. https://mashable.com/video/dahmer-monster-the-jeffrey-dahmer-story-trailer-netflix?utm_source=facebook&utm_medium=news_tab

Di Lillo, John. "Ben Crump's Quest for Justice Takes Center Stage in the New 'Civil' Trailer." Netflix, June 3, 2022. https://www.netflix.com/tudum/articles/watch-civil-trailer-ben-crump

Author Bio

My name is Wilkenson Francois. My previous marriage had afforded me the opportunity, as a father, to love and cherish two beautiful daughters, Genevieve (aged 8) and Esme (aged 6).

I emigrated from Haiti to Brooklyn, New York at age twelve. I attended my middle school at P.S. 398, The Walter Weaver Elementary School, and my high school at Samuel J. Tilden High School.

I made my way into college and graduated with an associate's degree in Electromechanical Engineering Technology (EMT) from New York City College of Technology (City Tech), as well as a bachelor's degree in Information Science and Technology (IS&T) from Temple University.

I am an immigrant, former documented alien, Haitian, and now a naturalized American citizen — U.S. Army Reserves, and a retired veteran. Ever since this unexplainable desire in me to pursue my education emerged, I got sucked into the world of cutting-edge technologies and have been associated with IT for some time. I continue to love the field even today, as I'm currently self-employed and running my own startup, called Lessimp, a dating platform.

It's my odyssey from a military man to an engineer to a matchmaker. I love to sleep, do karaoke, and sleep. I cannot stress enough the importance of sleep in my life as I am too busy chasing my dreams, especially now that you're reading my memoir.

In my fake heiress, Anna Sorokin, aka Anna Delvey's voice, "This whole story is completely true, except for all the parts that are totally made up." On a serious note, I enjoy riding my mini Jetson electric bike on the streets of the Williamsburg neighborhoods of Brooklyn, where I grew up. I currently reside in New York. Don't be surprised if you find me in any of the local bars in Brooklyn — you may even find yourself getting a beer on my tab.

www.ingramcontent.com/pod-product-compliance
Lightning Source LLC
Chambersburg PA
CBHW070724130626
46553CB00005B/2143